HOW TO WRITE

THE PERFECT PRESS RELEASE

HOW TO WRITE

THE PERFECT PRESS RELEASE

Real-life advice from editors
on getting your story in the media

PETER BARTRAM

A Helping Hand Book

from

New Venture Publishing

First published 2006 as a Helping Hand Book
by New Venture Publishing Ltd
© Peter Bartram 2006

New Venture Publishing Ltd
29 Tivoli Road, Brighton
East Sussex BN1 5BG

E-mail: info@newventurepublishing.co.uk
www.helpinghandbooks.co.uk

ISBN: 0-9552336-0-7
978-0-9552336-0-9

British Library cataloguing-in-publication data
A catalogue record for this book is obtainable from the British Library

Cover design by Mark Tennent
Typeset in Caslon by Mark Tennent, Worthing, West Sussex
Printed and bound by RPM Reprographics Ltd, Chichester, West Sussex

About the author

Peter Bartram is an experienced editor, business writer and journalist who has contributed to a wide range of newspapers and magazines. He wrote an earlier book on press release writing: *Writing a Press Release*. His other books include *Perfect Business Writing*, *The Perfect Report* and *The Perfect Project Manager* (all Random House Business Books).

CONTENTS

CHAPTER 1

START HERE

This is a book for people who want to get their company, their organisation, their leading personalities or their message into the media more often – and to do it in a way that generates coverage which helps them achieve their objectives.

There are many people for whom this activity is either a full-time obsession or a part-time distraction. They include the communications and public relations managers of companies large and small, the PR teams of government departments, local councils and a swathe of public bodies, consultants in professional PR firms, honorary officers in thousands of worthwhile voluntary organisations, elected politicians at all levels from MPs to councillors, not to mention a motley collection of professionals and celebrities – actors, lawyers, accountants, socialites. Even authors. In short, anyone with a product to sell, a service to provide, a message to proclaim – or a career to prop up.

We'll forget the last category, but in this book, we'll look at how to sell that product, provide that service or proclaim that message using the most basic PR tool of all – the press release.

Of course, the world of public relations and media coverage doesn't end with the press release. But it often starts with it. In skilled hands, a press release – or, as you might prefer to call it, a news release – can be a potent and effective way of generating media coverage. Every day, press releases are the source material for thousands of column centimetres in Britain's 11,000 newspapers and magazines. They also provide the raw material for hours of the spoken word on radio or television.

But there's a problem. A big one. Editors and broadcasters – in fact, pretty much all journalists – have an uneasy love-hate relationship with press releases. As we shall discover in the next chapter, around two in five journalists are willing to admit they have found a "really good" story from a press release at some time in their career. Some cheerfully own up to more than one really good story.

But to find that really good story, your average journalist has had to trawl through 215 press releases a week. Some get vastly more. In the course of researching this book I spoke to journalists who receive more than 500 releases a week and one editor who had to deal with 1,500. The vast bulk of those releases, say the journalists, are either irrelevant to their interests or contain no discernible story. So, to put it bluntly (and perhaps unkindly), from a journalist's point of view, hunting for a really good story among press releases is like searching for an orchid on a rubbish tip. As we shall see, most journalists are only able to find any kind of story in a very small percentage of the releases they receive.

In fact, the raw numbers of press releases which cascade into editors' inboxes puts into perspective just how difficult it is to get their attention – and why everything in the release you send has to be absolutely right. You may have lavished hours of work collecting information and drafting your release, but if it doesn't hit an editor's hot spot it won't even get read. You can tell the key that editors use to delete releases on their PCs – it's the worn-out one.

But your press release doesn't have to suffer that fate. This book starts from the premise that most PR people – whether they're full-time professionals or part-time amateurs – could make their press releases work harder for them by understanding more about what journalists want.

Just what do they want? How can a PR practitioner get a reputation for producing the kind of releases journalists actually take the trouble to read? In fact, is it possible to rehabilitate the much-maligned press release into a tool that PR people can use to serve their organisation's (or their client's) publicity objectives more effectively – and journalists accept more willingly?

If it is, there will be prizes all round. Prizes for PR people who will be able to focus their efforts more precisely to achieve better results for their organisations or clients. Prizes for journalists who will be more inclined to take a closer look at the releases which arrive by the hundreds in their e-mail inboxes, rather than reaching wearily yet again for that delete key.

During the course of researching this book, I collected the views of 89 editors and other journalists who, between them, receive more than 19,100 press releases a week. Or, to put it another way, 993,200 a year. The 89 include journalists who write for national newspapers and those who edit trade and technical journals. There are some from glossy bookstall magazines, some from local newspapers or regional magazines, others from the business and professional press. Most are staff journalists, a few are freelancers who contribute to many publications.

You'll be reading some of their opinions on what they like and don't like about press releases, starting in the next chapter. Their views have helped to shape the advice which follows in the rest of the book. (It's only fair to point out that even among journalists there are differences of detail about what constitutes good and bad practice in the writing and distribution of releases. In this book, I've tried to steer a middle course and present a consensus view which is, obviously, coloured by my own 30 years' experience in journalism.)

The strongest message that comes through from the journalists is that they want press releases to provide them with useful story ideas, which is not usually the case at the moment. But there is no reason why it shouldn't be if release writers start by addressing the six most common faults in releases (which we'll get to in chapter two), focus more on the readers they're trying to reach and tailor the information they provide to the journalists who receive it. For some press release writers that may mean just taking a more critical look at what they're doing and sharpening up their act. For others (and for beginners) it may mean going back to the basics of how to construct a release that will make an editor sit up and take notice. We'll look at a logical 14-step approach to writing the "perfect" press release in chapter eight.

The time and money spent writing and distributing press releases can deliver more helpful column inches if you master the basics. If you've already passed that base, you can improve your hit rate by applying some of the special tricks of the trade which make it much more likely that editors will want to use your release. (We'll look at some of those in chapters nine and 10.) You can almost certainly get better results with your press releases whether you're involved professionally in the world of public relations, write press releases for your company as a sideline to your regular work, or run a voluntary organisation that wants to grab its share of the headlines.

But I know from having spoken to hundreds of press release writers over the years that many are frustrated that their work doesn't get used more often. I've spoken to people who can't understand why their stories aren't picked up while a competitor seems to get acres of coverage. In just a few of these cases, the press release writers have unrealistic expectations. It's unlikely your press release is going to make the front page of a national newspaper, although plenty do make it into inside page stories. (And in the days when I was writing press releases, one made the front page lead in the Financial Times. I'll tell you more about that on page 110.)

The point is that by taking the advice from journalists that's scattered through these pages about what they want, you can improve the results you get from your press releases. That will improve the coverage your organisation gets in the media – and it won't do any harm to your reputation either.

By the time you reach the end of this book, I hope you will feel you've not only sharpened up your basic press release writing skills – or learnt them for the first time if you're new at the job – but that you've also discovered plenty of ideas you'd never previously considered that will help your organisation gain more press coverage.

That headline is only a good, well-written press release away.

CHAPTER 2

WHAT EDITORS THINK

When you send a press release to an editor or journalist you're adding to a flood that already pours into newspaper and magazine offices.

As we saw in the last chapter, the 89 editors and other journalists who contributed their views for this book receive between them around 19,100 press releases a week – an average of 215 each. But even that figure comes with a health warning. Most of those who replied gave an estimate which they admitted was on the low side. The true number could be more.

And the figure masks wide variations. Small specialist trade and technical magazines could be receiving as few as 20 or 30 a week. Others, notably business magazines, count (or should that be weigh?) their releases in the hundreds. On some newspapers and magazines, it's practically impossible to calculate the total number of releases that arrive because many go direct to individual writers rather than a central news desk.

Among my sample, 13 editors said they received 500 or more press releases a week (Table 1).

The figures are indicative of the sort of numbers similar publications are likely to receive. Thus, because Maxim Fashion receives around 1,000 releases a week, other leading bookstall titles will be in the same ballpark. Similarly, it is certainly not unusual for leading business titles to have more than 500 releases a week coming in. It has been impossible to discover a figure for any

national newspaper. It's clear hundreds of releases are received by
news desks, hundreds or even thousands more go straight to the
e-mail inboxes of department editors or specialist correspondents.

Table 1: Publications receiving more than 500 press releases a week

South East Business	1,500
Maxim Fashion	1,000
Mayfair Times	1,000
Food & Drink Network UK	900
Business Weekly	850
Director	750
Real Deals	700
Accountancy Age	500
Devon Today	500
Logistics Europe	500
Movie Club News	500
North Edinburgh News	500
North West Business Insider	500

Some of the editors who are deluged with releases don't hide
their irritation at the fact that many of the releases are not relevant.
John Harvey, editor of South East Business says he has never got a
really good story from a release. He says: "Many releases are riddled
with mistakes – they are written by people who have never been
journalists and go straight into PR from sub-standard creative and
media degree courses because the money is better."

Jenni Davies, editorial co-ordinator at Maxim Fashion, says:

"The main problem is filtering through junk/spam/bulk to find the ones which deserve to be read." At Mayfair Times, which has one of the most up-market readerships in Britain, Erik Brown says: "PR people don't appreciate the context in which we operate. We've had PRs incandescent with rage because we won't alter our editorial stance to their benefit – there has to be a local connection and a story that our readers would find interesting." And David Peasgood, who edits Food and Drink Network UK, says: "The most annoying of the lot are the faxed ones which are normally government generated and go straight in the bin without being read."

Table 2: Publications receiving fewer than 25 press releases a week

Operational Research Newsletter	25
Diabetes UK	20
Latest, The	20
Star	20
Somerset Life	15
Satra Bulletin International	10
Stamford Living	10

At the other end of the scale, there were seven publications that receive 25 or fewer releases a week (Table 2).

Clearly, the low numbers reflect the fact that most of these are niche publications, sometimes covering very specialised markets. But for some publications, even a handful of releases is too many. Although Pest Management Science receives only 30 releases a week, it uses none of them. Says editorial assistant Tom Hopkinson: "We are a peer review journal and do not publish news articles. Press releases go straight in the trash, so I guess from my point of view, the main fault is that people aren't making any effort to target their releases."

Apart from editors, freelance journalists are also on the receiving end of press releases, but they get far fewer, sometimes because they actively discourage them. Richard Willsher, the widely published financial journalist, gets about a 20 a week. He says: "I make it clear that I don't want to receive paper. I prefer to go and review relevant material online at a website." (We look at creating an online press release archive on page 147.) On the other hand, well-known IT writer Clive Couldwell receives 150 a week. He says: "PR people should refine their targeting and find out what I require. Only two companies have contacted me this year to ask."

Freelancer Jim Mortleman takes a hard line with unwanted press releases. He says: "Most of the releases that I still receive are picked up and automatically deleted by my spam filter these days, so I'm not sure how many I'm actually sent. The only ones that now get through are those from PRs I trust and have included as exceptions in my spam-filtering rules! As a freelance writer (mainly doing feature work) I've been fairly proactive at telling PR people to take me off their bulk mailing lists, and I let very few PRs have my postal mailing address. I used to receive in the region of 100-200 a week by e-mail, I guess, of which I'd maybe read two or three a day that seemed of interest. When I was a full-time editor, however, the number was ridiculous – probably about 250 paper releases a day and a similar number by e-mail."

Dominic Roskrow, who edits four bi-monthly magazines at Paragraph Publishing, including the promisingly named Whisky

Magazine, points out the kind of long odds PR people face when they send a press release. "I get about 300 releases a week, mainly by e-mail. But I have 24 magazines a year and each contains 20 news stories. So that's 480 releases from a total of 15,000." That's worse than 30-1 – and other magazines offer even longer odds.

And there are plenty of problems that could make your release a rank outsider.

HOW PRESS RELEASES ARE USED

Most of them are never used. A goodly number are never even read. The 89 editors and journalists who took part in the survey will, on average, use eight per cent as a story in its own right, although often heavily rewritten and shortened. But that figure varies widely from one publication to another.

Of the thousand releases that turn up each week at Maxim Fashion, just one might make it into a story. At Director – where, according to editor Joanna Higgins, of a typical week's 750 releases "70 per cent don't even bear opening" – one or two might make it into their own story. None of the 500 releases which arrive at Logistics Europe will do so. Steve Hughes, editor of the Bolton Evening News, uses "hardly any" of his week's allotment of more than 200 releases as a stand-alone story. "We pass quite a few on to our advertising department as sales leads, as much of the information provided is not news at all," he adds.

At the other end of the scale, some chiefly trade and technical publications make higher use of their releases. Editor Andrew Gibbs uses around 75 per cent of the 150 releases he receives at monthly magazine Business MK, which circulates in the Milton Keynes area. At Diabetes UK, managing editor Martin Cullen uses around 70 per cent of a week's 20 releases. And editor Jackie

Stokes may use as much as 60 per cent of her weekly complement of 50 releases for Aer Arann in-flight magazine, Express It. Overall, only nine of the 89 journalists say they get stand-alone stories from more than 10 per cent of the releases they receive.

But if your release doesn't make it immediately into print, there is at least a chance it could be used as background for another story or as an idea for a future piece. On average, the 89 journalists use 7.3 per cent of releases for background while 6.1 per cent of them stimulate ideas for another story.

Even if your release doesn't get used in any way, it's still possible that it might play some useful role. Quite a few journalists – including Richard Young, editor of Real Finance and Katherine Simmons at Surrey Life – identify useful future contacts from the information on them. Some, including Jane MacArthur, editor at Blackhair, may ring up contacts on releases for quotes on another story. Others, including Ato Erzan-Essien, editor of Big Issue in the North, and Lorie Church, editor of In and Around Covent Garden, pull information off releases for magazine listings. But the editor of a famous financial title adds: "About one per cent get passed around the office because they are so comically ridiculous."

SIX MAIN FAULTS IN PRESS RELEASES

Why is it that so many press releases end up in the bin rather than in the paper? The 89 editors and other journalists who took part in the survey voted on six key faults which turn them off of using potential stories.

Fault 1: irrelevant to their interests

The greatest of these faults is that the release is irrelevant to their interests – 72 of the journalists (81%) said this was a fault compared with eight (9%) who didn't see it as a problem and nine (10%) who had no view either way. (Percentages may not equal 100% because of rounding.) Time and again, editors have complained to me that PR people are not taking the time to study the interests of the publications they're bombarding with press releases. As a result, editors have to wade through hundreds of releases merely to find those that might possibly make a story. No wonder the delete button is working overtime in editorial inboxes.

Andrew Sawers, editor of Financial Director, says: "Irrelevance is a major fault." Andy, who receives more than 250 releases a week, adds: "It's too easy to send press releases, therefore everyone sends them to everyone." Laurence Watts, editor of North Norfolk-based Town & Country News, who receives more than 100 releases a week, says: "In the majority of cases, this is why they are not used."

Fault 2: no story or weak story

Almost as big a problem – mentioned by 70 (79%) of the journalists – is the fact that too many releases have no story or only a weak one. But 12 (14%) of the journalists didn't see this as a problem and seven (8%) expressed no view either way.

A common complaint is that releases simply contain material which is designed to promote the company concerned without any pretence of providing a news hook. But as several of the editors have pointed out, promotional material is not a story – it's an advertisement. Perhaps this is why on some publications, a number of releases get passed to the ad team as sales leads.

The failure to provide a clear story is an endemic fault. Terry Fletcher, editor in chief of a group of regional magazines including Countryman and Dalesman, has awarded the Chocolate Digestive in his "Well, that takes the biscuit" worst press release awards to a release from a college about a new course. Says Terry: "Having read it twice, I've no idea what it's about, but the college is teaching unspecified skills, to unspecified people to take advantage of unspecified opportunities thanks to a learning environment that is unique in some unspecified way." You don't need to read the release to tell from Terry's analysis just what was wrong with it – and, indeed, too many other releases that waffle in a generalised way. Hard facts and sharp angles make news.

Fault 3: self-promotion or puffery

Hot on the heels of the first two faults – and mentioned as a problem by 68 (76%) of the journalists – is self-promotion or puffery. But 15 (17%) weren't concerned by this and six (7%) had no view. As one or two journalists point out, it's quite natural that organisations should want to speak highly of themselves. But what they fail to appreciate is that most newspapers and magazines simply aren't going to publish self-praise.

Of course, journalists can chop out the offending phrases and rewrite the copy, but that's extra work in what will probably be a busy editorial office. For a release that's teetering on the margins of being used or not, that extra work may well tip it towards the bin. Nicholas Rudd-Jones, publisher of a string of magazines including Stamford Living and Essential Living, complains that too many of the releases he receives require "massive editing" to make them suitable for publication. "Why can't they be written in ordinary everyday English and focus on facts?" he laments.

Fault 4: poor English

Among the survey journalists, 46 (52%) were troubled by poor

English in press releases. But the problem didn't bother 36 (40%) of the journalists, while seven (8%) had no view. Among those not troubled were editors who said they'd come to expect poor English and it was, after all, their job to correct it.

Much depends on what counts as poor English. Certainly, elementary grammatical errors are endemic in releases. They even creep into headlines as in: "Knowledge College respond to a changing rural environment". (Singular subject, plural verb.) But, more generally, too many releases are written in a stilted and over-formal style. As one editor notes, vocabulary is often limited – "emphatic nuance can be achieved through a considered choice of words". Another mentions the lack of richness and colour in the way information is presented. But there's an alternative danger: going over the top with too much florid writing.

Fault 5: confusing jargon

This was named as a fault by 44 (49%) of the journalists. It wasn't a problem for 37 (42%) and eight (9%) had no view. It's a problem which is unevenly distributed. Editors operating in the business, trade and technical press are far more likely to complain about jargon than journalists in other fields.

Unfortunately, it's clear that there are still too many PR people out there who greatly over-estimate the knowledge level of readers of even quite technical publications. To compound the problem, they then send releases for technical journals to non-technical publications. What, for example, was Andy Sawers, editor of Financial Director, to make of the following opening sentence from a release he received?

"Gobbledygook Systems Inc. (Nasdaq: AAAGH!), the leading provider of open software products and services for the communications industry, today announced that over 12 million subscribers are now using Gobbledygook's WAP 2.0 technology via KDDI's "au" branded 3G mobile phone services (CDMA 1X and CDMA 1X WIN) based on CDMA2000 1x and CDMA 2000 1x EV-DO technology." (Name of company changed to protect the guilty.)

Perhaps there is a story here. Perhaps somebody on a technical journal would understand what's going on. But the editor of a financial magazine couldn't reasonably be expected to do so. In any event, if there is a story, it would be much clearer if told in plain English.

In general terms, there could be two reasons for excessive recourse to jargon. One is that PR people's clients insist on including it. They should be told that they are doing themselves no favours and that they're reducing, by a substantial factor, the chances of seeing their story in print. The second is that it masks a lack of understanding by the writer. It's easier to fall back on jargon when you've not fully grasped the meaning of what you're writing. But that's not what the best writing in any genre is about – it ought to be about communicating meaning.

Fault 6: too long

Of the editors and journalists in the survey, 37 (42%) found press releases too long and 42 (47%) didn't – a narrow majority against. The remaining 10 (11%) had no view. But even some of those editors who were laid back about length, weren't fussed about it because they found releases easy to cut. In practice, few if any releases get published at full length and most would benefit from careful editing to cut out marginal matter and to ensure that what's left is written in the most succinct way.

In fact, there's a wider problem – a paradox. Many releases are too long but they don't contain enough information. That's because the writers haven't focused on what information it is that the readers of the target publications will really want to know about. Fiona Armstrong, at Best Scottish Weddings (80 releases a week), sums up the dilemma: "Length can be a problem – a release is often too long, but then it totally depends on what you might use it for. Sometimes there is a need for more detail."

Other faults that journalists hate

Apart from the six main faults, journalists have a long list of things they hate. High on that list are follow-up phone calls. "Nothing is more deeply irritating than PRs ringing up to ask if you received a press release, if you liked it, plan to use it, etc," says Susi Rogol at Bridal Buyer. "I hate being followed up by PRs to check that the release arrived," says Sophie Chalmers at Better Business. "If we're not going to use the story, no amount of follow-up will make any difference." Louise Taylor, deputy editor of Cheshire Life, is another journalist who could do with fewer follow-up calls. "I politely express lack of interest and then I get a call three days later by someone else in their office asking me the same questions," she says. Louise adds: "If I'm interested in the story, I'll get back to them. If I say, 'sorry, it's not really our thing', they ought to believe that I know what I'm talking about."

Poor timing is another issue high on editors' hate lists. It's annoying for them to receive a story they might have used had it turned up before deadline. By the next issue, it will probably be too old to use. "The longer lead times of a monthly are rarely taken into consideration," says Joanna Higgins, editor of Director. Richard Maynard, at Newbury Business News, complains of "too short notice of time-sensitive stories, not taking into account the deadlines or publication dates of a particular organisation".

Next on the hate list: pointless quotes. Too many of them are just empty words – others merely repetitious. Ross Butler, editor of Real Deals, sums up the problem: "Quotes by key people in press releases are almost always meaningless. They nearly always vapidly repeat what has already been asserted. The worst is when these people are merely quoted as saying how happy they are about the event in question. Nobody cares. Either say something that is worthwhile or leave it out." (We look at how to write quotes that work on page 114.)

E-mailed press releases are a firm bone of contention with many journalists. Richard Young, editor at Real Finance, points out: "E-mail releases are often over-formatted. PR people stick in huge numbers of line returns between paragraphs making the release difficult to read and even worse to print out. They'll think they're being clever with massive headline fonts or lots of italicisation. But the recipient's e-mail system usually makes this look different (or worse) to how it looked to the sender." John Scrimshaw, managing editor of Fashion Business International, adds: "Most releases these days come by e-mail, which is fine. But some PRs don't seem to understand the point of e-mail, which is to make the text instantly accessible. There's increasing use of PDF files, which have no advantages except that they look pretty. I even get some press releases as jpeg attachments containing images of scanned print. If it has to be re-keyed or won't copy and paste properly, it will probably go to the bottom of the pile."

Other hates include releases with missing details (including who to contact for further information), e-mailed stories with too many attachments – and sending the release to the wrong person. "We still receive press releases for people who left the company years ago," says Cassie Steer at Marie Claire. "It just looks a bit unprofessional." Indeed it does.

Many of the problems with press releases would be avoided if – as Damian Wild, editor of Accountancy Age, points out – PR people thought about why the readers of a particular title would be interested in their announcement. "You should ask yourself the question: 'would I read a paper that carried this announcement if I wasn't being paid to do so?'"

The good news

Yet despite all the hates, some journalists acknowledge that they have found a good story in a release from time to time. Of the 89 editors and journalists, 38 (43%) said they had found a "really good" story in a press release. Of the others, 23 (26%) denied they'd ever found a good story, and 28 (32%) provided no answer to this question, which probably means they've never found a "really good" story or they would have mentioned it. Some editors said that, by definition, they would never find a "really good" story in a release, simply because it wouldn't be exclusive or "off diary" – a story which they'd researched from their own contacts.

Yet quirky off-beat stories, cleverly presented, sometimes get big coverage in national newspapers. Freelancer Jim Mortleman recalls a story he wrote about a small IT security company which had put out a release claiming that hackers could tap into London companies' wireless IT networks using empty Pringles cans. Explains Jim: "They followed it up by taking a bunch of journalists round the City in a minibus to show it could be done. This resulted in coverage in several national newspapers and BBC Online. As a freelance, I fleshed out the story by tracking down and speaking to a campaigning wireless hacker and managed to flog the story to The Guardian. This, in turn, gave me the idea to do another piece on community wireless networks, which I also flogged to The Guardian."

Allison Heller, deputy editor at Housebuilder, is another journalist who has mined the press release pile for good stories. "There have been a number," she says. "Often they are a quirky angle, very well researched or contain statistical or survey information that points out interesting trends."

But good stories, even when they exist, don't necessarily hit editors between the eyes. "The skill is seeing the angle in the words that no-one else will go for to get you away from the rest of the pack," says David Bennett, at Southampton City View magazine.

One journalist who spotted a worthwhile story hidden in the verbiage was freelancer Annie Roberts, who edits lifestyle magazines. The story was about reuniting a sister, who was adopted when her mother died, with her other brothers and sisters. It was tucked away in a release appealing for more adoptive parents. Another example of how a story can sometimes lie behind the story in the press release comes from Karen Murray at Scottish Health News. "I got a release on a new cream for the treatment of psoriasis, which became an interesting article on the person who invented it," she recalls.

But, as Katherine Simmons, editor of Surrey Life, points out, the good stories tend to come from "the press officers that read the magazine regularly and, on that basis, make relevant suggestions to the magazine and its readership. As a result, they have built up a good working relationship. For example, this morning a press officer has just phoned me from one of our racecourses offering a 'behind the scenes' feature on a busy race day – perfect for our readers. The press officer concerned has actually thought beyond the organisation she is representing to what would interest the readers of Surrey Life. Too often PRs don't consider whether or not they are putting out something that is of interest or benefit to the reader. Usually though, if it's a good enough story and they've built up a good relationship, they won't wait to write a release, they'll just phone to pitch it."

For Sue Copeman, editor of StrategicRISK, a trade journal focusing on risk management, press releases sometimes provide a trigger for a feature. Explains Sue: "We don't have a big staff so rely a lot on external contributors. Releases can often trigger an idea for a feature which we commission the issuer to write. With the right brief, most of the features I've commissioned in this way have been really good."

Finally, Jenni Davies, editorial co-ordinator at Maxim Fashion, points out that a release can sometimes turn into a special piece of editorial. "I was sent a release on a company which performs revolutionary hair transplant operations," she recalls. "That has resulted in us running a competition for readers to win a new set of hair! All they had to do was send us a picture and tell us why they deserve not to be bald."

So you want to know how to write releases which make stories that editors really want? The first step is to find out more about what makes news.

CHAPTER 3

HITTING THE HEADLINES

Some organisations make it into the media all the time – but wish they didn't. They're in the papers or on the television for all the wrong reasons – because journalists are reporting bad news about them. It's important to understand that, on the whole, journalists are going to write about your organisation in the way they see it, irrespective of whether they believe it will be helpful or not to you.

The point about putting out press releases (or any other public relations activity, for that matter) is to provide a flow of information that is helpful to your organisation and which can also provide journalists with useful copy. After all, journalists may well receive information about your organisation from unhelpful sources. These could include dissatisfied customers looking to make trouble, so-called independent consultants hoping to make a name for themselves, academic commentators with an axe to grind, and competitors eager to queer your pitch. The least you owe to your own organisation is to generate a steady flow of "good news" which presents what you're doing in a favourable light.

The problem with many smaller organisations – whether companies or voluntary sector bodies – is that they don't always realise that they are sitting on a whole raft of good news stories. So the first issue we need to explore is where those stories are – and what makes them of potential interest to journalists.

The nature of news

What is news?

Over the years, various notable editors and writers have had their stab at defining it. The American journalist John B Bogart famously remarked: "When a dog bites a man that is not news, but when a man bites a dog that is news." In Britain, Hilaire Belloc, best known as author of *The Cautionary Tales*, said: "Journalism largely consists of saying 'Lord Jones is dead' to people who never knew Lord Jones was alive."

Newspaper proprietor, the original Lord Northcliffe, equated news with revelation: "News is what somebody somewhere wants to suppress; all the rest is advertising." More formally, the *Oxford English Dictionary*, defines news as "new or fresh information; reports of what has most recently happened". We get closer to understanding the nature of modern-day news when we come to Harold Evans, the legendary former editor of The Sunday Times. He wrote in his *The Practice of Journalism*: "News is people. It is people talking and people doing. Committees and Cabinets and courts are people; so are fires, accidents and planning decisions. They are only news because they involve and affect people." And reinforcing that theme, Arthur Christensen, the greatest editor of the Daily Express, advised his reporters: "Always, always, always tell the story through people."

There is a common theme in most of these ideas and it is this – news is something that somebody somewhere could be interested in learning about. That is a fact you need to keep right at the front of your mind when you think about the news potential of your own organisation.

What's more important than general theories about news, is how news actually works in newspapers and magazines. Understanding this provides a framework for thinking about the kind of news you might have within your own organisation.

In broad outline, journalists tend to think about news in two ways:

Hard or soft

The first way is whether an item is hard news or soft news. Hard news is something of immediate and urgent importance. It needs to go into the first issue of the publication available – next day's newspaper in the case of a daily – or on the first available news bulletin on television or radio. At its most dramatic, hard news is about the resignation of governments, the crashing of aeroplanes, the outbreak of wars. But it's also about the divorce of a celebrity, the transfer of a famous footballer, the winning numbers in the National Lottery.

But hard news doesn't need to be of national importance. The key factor from a journalist's point of view is that people need to know about it straight away. If they don't, readers, listeners or viewers will find out about it from some other source and the news will become stale. The publication will look inept because it has missed the story.

You may think that you don't have hard news in your organisation, but it's quite possible that you do. If you're a quoted company on the stock exchange, the announcement of your financial results is a hard news item. If you're a voluntary organisation, the election of a prominent personality as your next president could be hard news for the local paper. The point here is that if you have a hard news story which you want to put in a press release, you need to do it straight away to ensure that it reaches the very next edition of the publication you're aiming at. Hard news is perishable. Leave it untouched and, like milk allowed to stand, it will go off and become unusable.

Soft news is different because it's not so time sensitive. A soft news story could be about the plans an MP has to campaign on an issue of public concern, the reasons why an author decided to write her new book, or the company chairman's speech on how the market for widgets will develop in the next two years. Although soft news is not so time-sensitive as hard news, it still needs to be topical. But it often consists of the kind of story that won't lose too much if it waits until the next issue of a newspaper or magazine. Although a soft news story will still be driven by facts, it may not have quite such a hard edge as the hard news story. In the soft news story, there may be more room for opinion and speculation.

Many organisations have plenty of soft news stories if only they knew where to look for them. They are the kind of stories which, if presented with skill, can help to round out an organisation's image in a favourable light. The work that a director does with the charity for disabled children, the machine shop engineer's idea which is saving the company £100,000 a year, the training scheme which is developing women business leaders are just three (from potentially hundreds) of the sort of ideas that make soft news stories.

Diary and off-diary stories

Another way journalists think about news is as diary or off-diary stories. It is useful for press release writers to know how this distinction works because, while journalists are looking for both kinds, they are often very keen to find off-diary stories which their rivals haven't got. It's the off-diary stories which give a newspaper or magazine its distinctive personality and the editorial edge that it enjoys over rivals.

A diary story is, quite simply, a story that's flagged in the news room's diary. It's any event which journalists know is going to take place and which might provide stories that are worth writing about. Such events run from sittings of parliament, courts and local councils through to annual general meetings of companies and scheduled sporting events. Much of the news coverage of national, regional and local newspapers is planned around diary stories. Many magazines also carry diary stories in their news pages.

But it's because everybody knows about diary stories, that journalists are especially keen to discover off-diary stories – which, they hope, only they know about. Off-diary stories may be the result of their private research, a tip-off – or even a press release. Some of the 89 journalists who took part in this book's survey mentioned they had found useful off-diary stories for their publications. Three examples are a story about a Briton trapped in Guantanamo Bay (city magazine), a TV star who was unexpectedly involved with a local charity (local newspaper), a castle that was hiring its first court jester for 300 years (business magazine).

FIVE TESTS FOR ANY STORY

Whether hard or soft, on-diary or off-diary, there are five key tests you ought to apply to any story that you plan to issue in a press release. These are:

Relevance

The story needs to be relevant to the publications or broadcasters you plan to send it to. This may sound obvious. Sadly, every day hundreds and possibly thousands of press releases are sprayed out across the media with little consideration as to whether the overwhelmed journalists on the receiving end of this literary tidal wave will find the information of any use.

This has two bad effects. First, it makes all journalists wary about all press releases. If the proportion of irrelevant press releases is too high, they may choose not to read any of them. Or, at any rate, only give them the most cursory of glances. Second, if the particular journalists you are trying to target believe you're bombarding them with too much irrelevant material, you may turn them off when you actually have a story they might find of interest. Key lesson: be sure you only send a press release to journalists who are likely to find it of value.

Timeliness

If you have a piece of news, send it as soon as you can. Don't sit on a good story believing that it may mature like a fine wine. As we've already noted, the reverse is the case. And although hard news deteriorates faster than soft news, both soon slip across that fine line which divides news from history. One reason why stories sometimes limp into newspaper offices days or even weeks too late is that PR people have been hoping there's a "right moment" from their organisation's point of view when their announcement would make the best news. Another is that press officers aren't familiar with the deadlines of the publications they're dealing with so that releases turn up too late to be included in the current edition – and are too old by the time the next comes round. This is a problem for weekly newspapers and magazines and even more so for monthly magazines. Sections of magazines are prepared for printers as much as three or four weeks before they appear on news stands or drop through subscribers' letterboxes. Key lesson: find out deadlines for key publications and make sure you hit them with as much margin to spare as you can provide.

Readable

This ought to go without saying, but sadly too many press releases fall far short of what journalists are looking for. It's not just that the story – if there is one – is hidden away somewhere on the second page. (Journalists will soon realise they're wasting their time on the first page and won't reach the second.) It's also that too many releases are littered with elementary grammatical and spelling errors. Maybe they don't always obscure the meaning, but they create an appearance of amateurishness – even sloppiness – and journalists reading the release may think that if the writers can't get simple details right, can they get anything right?

Focused

But to make a journalist sit up and take notice, the release needs to be more than a readable ramble through a topic of interest to you and your organisation. Instead, it needs to be focused on to the concerns of the publications or broadcast programmes at which it's targeted. That means you need to know the kinds of issues that are currently on the minds of the journalists who work for your target publications – the sort of subjects they're writing about, even the hot topics that are making news. Then your release needs to be crafted so that it's designed to hit the journalist's hot button. We'll be looking in detail at how you can craft your release in this way in chapter nine. Key lesson: focus your press release so that journalists can see it's relevant to subjects they're likely to be writing about

Presentable

Finally, it needs to be presentable. If you're sending it as a printed release through the post – and many are still sent out this way – you need to ensure that it's legibly printed and adheres to all the points of presentation which we'll look at on page 140. If you're sending it by e-mail – as the vast majority of press releases now are – you need to be certain that it's in a format which is acceptable to the publication concerned. (We'll look at e-mailed releases in more detail on page 141.) Key lesson: present your release in such a way that journalists will find it easy and helpful to access and use.

Understanding news values

I'm regularly rung up by press officers to ask whether a press release they sent me has been used. Sometimes I get an e-mail asking the same question. Similar calls and e-mails are received in newspaper and magazine offices up and down the country to the mounting rage of most editors. Apart from the fact that fielding these calls or answering the e-mails is an irritating distraction for busy working journalists – there are press cutting services which will monitor news coverage on behalf of anybody who cares to pay them (see page 162) – the calls indicate that the PRs in question haven't really understood the news values of the publications they're targeting. If they did, they wouldn't need to ask whether the release they've sent is of any interest.

It's important to try to understand the news values of the publications you want to target. The reason for this is that news values play an important role in influencing both the subjects which the publication (or the tv or radio programme) chooses to cover and the way in which it deals with the topic. In most cases, the news values are influenced by the readership or by the perceived interests and attitudes of readers the publication wishes to attract.

In some cases, publications wear their news values – like their hearts – on their sleeves. Compare, for example, two national newspapers, the Daily Mail (socially conservative) and The Guardian (socially liberal). The Daily Mail gives considerable prominence to coverage of issues that interest women, reflecting its strong circulation among ABC1 category females. The Guardian is widely read by people who work in public service – central or local government – which is reflected in the substantial supplements devoted to issues such as education and social work every week. Most publications, whether national papers or more local or specialised titles, have developed their own editorial values.

If you are embarking on a public relations campaign for the first time, it is important to study the news values of the publications or programmes that will be your prime targets. Look for themes which occur regularly and study how they are reflected in the choice of subject matter. Look particularly at who is asked to contribute information or quotes to articles. Think about whether you can provide similar information from your organisation or whether you can develop a spokesperson in your organisation whom journalists will approach for comments.

It's important to realise that the question of news values tends to permeate most publications in one way or another. That includes local and regional newspapers as well as consumer magazines and the business, trade and technical press. Sometimes what passes for news values is little more than a prejudice in favour of covering a particular subject or, perhaps, just a hobby-horse. Whatever they are, understanding them is like creeping inside journalists' minds and once you understand how they work, you're part of the way to writing a press release that can make it into print.

WHAT HAPPENS TO PRESS RELEASES?

The short answer: most of them are binned.

But don't give up. If you understand a little more about what journalists do when they receive a press release, yours is less likely to end up in the bin. In fact, that could be a personal computer desktop cyberbin these days as most press releases are e-mailed to their recipients.

Every publication has its own procedures but, in broad outline, this is what will happen on different kinds of publications. On national and regional newspapers, releases that aren't sent to a specific individual are routed to the news room where they'll be briefly looked at by a "copy taster". In the case of a national, the copy taster might be full-time, while on a regional paper he or she may be doubling up the job with other duties.

Whichever is the case, the copy taster will be looking to see whether the release is likely to contain a story the paper might want to publish or whether it ought to be routed to one of the paper's specialist reporters – for example, for business, sport, travel, motoring and so on. A lot of the obvious dross will head straight for the bin at this stage. Some of the releases will be routed for further consideration to another reporter.

On magazines, releases may first pass over the desk, or through the PC, of either the editor or the news editor, depending on the size of the publication and the number of staff it has. Either will be searching for a relevant story that will fit into the next or a future issue.

On local newspapers, releases will probably go straight to the news editor who will perform the copy tasting job and either bin them or route them on to reporters as appropriate. In many cases on national, regional and local newspapers as well as magazines, releases may be sent direct to individual reporters thought to be interested in the topic or to specialist correspondents. (We shall look at the targeting of press releases further on page 69.)

Wherever the release finally ends up, one of five things is likely to happen to it:

1 The release may be rewritten as a story and appear in the paper. (Go to page 82 to find a 14-step approach to writing press releases that get used.)

2 The release may be filleted for a quote or a snippet of information which may appear in a story the journalist is already working on. (Go to page 114 to find out how to include quotable quotes in press releases.)

3 The release may be filed by the journalist for use in a future story or as background information. (Go to page 102 to find out how you can tailor your release so that it might get used immediately.)

4 You may be rung up and asked for further information. Depending on whether the journalist finds what you tell him helpful or not, the release may then be treated in one of the first three ways. (Go to page 143 to find out how to deal with a call from a journalist.)

5 The release may be dumped in the bin. (Return to page 1 and start re-reading this book to prevent this disaster.)

LAYING GROUNDWORK FOR SUCCESS

Why is it our competitors always get in the press (or on the television and radio) and we don't?

That's a question that often gets asked of PR people by managing directors, chairmen and others leading organisations which aren't getting the media coverage they think they warrant.

Perhaps, not surprisingly, those competitors will also be asking the same question of their own hapless press officer, for media coverage tends to stimulate selective vision in those who are written about (or not written about). The excellent article on page seven is overshadowed by the competitor's mention on page 19. Or the quote from the rival chairman is three lines longer than the one from your own – no matter that your own chairman's is patently more pertinent and interesting.

It is the luckless task of the publicist to deal with the imagined slights created by the selective vision of those who direct their organisation. But you can minimise the problem both by developing a more effective approach to press releases (and other aspects of the publicity campaign) and by creating the right framework for the writing and distribution of press releases in the first place. Even before you start tapping out your first release, this is an issue you need to resolve.

Chapter 4

Setting ground rules

So far, I've been rather tough on press release writers. I've accused them, inter alia, of sending out press releases without sensible stories and annoying journalists with time-wasting phone calls.

But there's another side to the coin. And if you're already responsible for writing press releases inside an organisation, you'll know what it is. You have to deal with the complex ebb and flow of power politics within the organisation, not to mention the kaleidoscopic cast of characters, all of whom have their own ideas about what information should be sent out as a press release and how it should be written. While nobody would tell the financial director how to present the accounts or the logistics director how to distribute the products, everybody, it sometimes seems, believes they have a right, if not a duty, to tell the press officer how to draft the press releases.

Let us be clear. It is quite proper – indeed, essential – that any organisation should develop a policy about how information is written and released to the press. (In a few moments, we will discuss how that policy might be framed.) But once the policy is in place, the press officer should be allowed to get on with his or her job in a professional manner. The kind of detailed day-to-day interference in the drafting minutiae of press releases – except in special cases, such as where there may be legal doubts or a financial dimension with stock market implications – undermines the professionalism of press officers, saps their creative juices and destroys their confidence in their ability (if not their will to live!). Which means that a successful publicist needs, besides an eye for a story and the way with words needed to turn it into lively copy, the tact of a diplomat, the resolve of a general, the patience of a saint – and, not infrequently, the weasely cunning of a politician.

Putting a policy in place

There are, essentially, only three key elements in a press release policy for an organisation, although their complexity varies considerably depending on the size and nature of the organisation. The three elements are (1) who is responsible for drafting releases and sending them to the media, (2) who is responsible for approving the draft of releases before they are sent to the media and (3) what are the responsibilities of other people in the organisation to provide information that is needed for the media relations campaign. Let's look in general terms at how you might manage those issues in a large organisation, such as a big multinational company or a major government department, a medium-sized organisation such as a private company or a small public body, and a small organisation, such as a small firm or local charity, where both professional and voluntary staff work side-by-side or where all the participants are part-time volunteers.

Very large organisation

If you work in a very large organisation, such as a multinational company, the media relations policy will probably be controlled at board level through either the marketing director or a specialist communications director. In the case of some elements of the policy, such as financial matters and relations with the market, the financial director, chief executive and, conceivably, the chairman will be involved at a policy level.

The communications director may sit on the board but, if not, report to the board through the marketing director or possibly one of the other directors such as the chief executive. The communications director will probably manage a significant central public relations staff. In the case of decentralised organisations, some PR staff may be devolved to look after specific divisions or overseas subsidiary companies. In this case, the organisation chart will look like a classic pyramid structure with press officers reporting up to a communications director at the top of the pyramid.

In this situation, there will probably be a policy about what kind of material can be issued to the press at divisional and subsidiary level and what is reserved for the top. The communications director will almost certainly reserve financial reporting for the top together with issues such as board changes, mergers and acquisitions, disposals, major new policies, such as shift in strategy and other similar matters. Divisions and subsidiaries will probably handle matters such as their own key appointments, new product announcements, customer wins and so on. Whether or not divisions or subsidiaries need to get releases cleared at the top largely depends on how much autonomy the company as a whole wants to give to divisions. In other words, it's a matter of broader management style. But whatever the detail, the overall picture is one of clear levels of responsibility and reporting chains, with those at lower levels of the chain having a clear understanding of matters that should be reported upwards before being issued to the press.

In large organisations, there may sometimes be a case for press releases to be checked by the company's lawyers before they're released. This certainly applies to releases dealing with certain financial matters, to regulatory issues or to releases

which are responding to accusations made against the company
(for example, about an unsafe product or a breach of health and
safety laws). Whatever the precise details, it is important that the
policies are written down and that everybody who works in press
relations knows what they are. This includes PR consultancies
that supplement the work of the in-house press officers. Although
consultants may help in drafting and distributing releases, they
should always refer both the text and distribution list to the in-
house team so that they can be sanctioned at the relevant levels in
the chain of command before material goes to journalists.

Medium-sized organisation

A medium-sized organisation will often try to apply a cut-down
version of the management and approval process adopted in a large
organisation. That's fine as far as it goes, but there are a couple of
contradictory dangers to watch out for.

The first is trying to replicate too much of a large organisation's
management process. If you have too many people involved, you'll
merely create a bureaucracy that will slow down the whole press
relations campaign. Moreover, you'll also create a situation where
people on the fringe of the process will try to leverage what little
influence they have over it by raising trivial points. I'm thinking
here of the sort of people who go to committee meetings and whose
only contribution is to point out that there's a comma missing on
page three of the minutes. You certainly need to proofread your
press releases – we'll come to that on page 128 – but you don't
want marginal interferons gumming up the works.

The other problem is the reverse side of the coin. Because
you're a medium-sized organisation, you may concentrate the
management and review process in too few hands. This can lead

to two effects that hold back the media campaign. First, because not enough people are involved, the flow of information on which good story-based press releases depend, dries up. Secondly, sooner or later you will issue a release that will legitimately upset a manager in another part of the organisation for a reason you hadn't anticipated.

At the end of the day, it all comes down to a question of balance. You need to involve those people in the organisation who are likely to be strong sources of information for press releases or who have major management responsibility for the subjects dealt with in your releases.

As a medium-sized organisation, it's probable that you won't have such a diverse structure as a large organisation, so the problem of satellite press officers reporting into the centre may not arise. But if it does, the same broad principles as those used in the larger organisation apply.

Small organisation

You might think that it would be easiest to deal with the questions of management and approval of press releases in a small organisation. But, then, if you work in a small organisation – either as an employee or as a volunteer in a charitable or community body – you will know that's not necessarily the case.

One reason is that when an organisation is small, formal management structures tend to disappear in favour of informal networks of people. (It's worth mentioning, as an aside, that informal networks also work in large and medium-sized organisations alongside the formal management structures.) However, in small organisations, the informal networks are more important.

At one level, that can be helpful when you're running a media relations campaign. Because everybody knows everybody else's business, it's easier to get hold of the information you need for your press release. In theory, at least. You may still meet awkward individuals who don't want to help you with media relations, either because they think it's a waste of time or because they wish they were running it instead of you – as it's more interesting than their own work.

But at another level, it might prove more difficult. Because everybody knows everybody else's business, you must remember that they will know yours. Because what you do has an impact on the way your organisation is portrayed in the media, they'll be especially interested in what you do. Expect to get much unwanted advice and offers of help from people who are just dying to do the job themselves. Of course, it's wise to take good advice. But much of the advice you'll get in this situation won't be good – and some may be downright bad.

So to be successful at handling press relations in a small organisation, you need to be skilled in the craft of relationship management. Your smiling disposition to keep everybody happy will mask a granite will which, at the same time, ensures that everything gets done in the way that delivers the best results.

The precise details of the approval process in a small organisation obviously depend on the size and purpose of the organisation. In a small organisation, it's likely that the managing director (or, possibly, the marketing/sales director) will be the fount of approval. In a voluntary organisation, the chairman may approve press releases before they are issued to the media. He or she may choose to involve selected other individuals on a case by case basis, depending on the nature of the release.

It is not, however, unknown in some voluntary organisations for press releases to be the subject of full-scale debates at committee meetings. On rare occasions, when the release concerns a matter of major policy, which is going to affect the way people perceive the organisation, this might be acceptable. Too often, however, such debates merely provide an argument over words. It's an occasion where the pedants come into their own and the individual who discovered the missing comma on page three of the last meeting's minutes finds a new purpose in life. If you come up against this situation, you have two choices. Either you can invite the committee to adopt a more streamlined approach to approving press releases (perhaps involving the chairman and yourself) or you can resign.

BULLDOZING THE ROAD BLOCKS

Not every person in every organisation is enthusiastic about publicising its activities in the media. When it comes to companies, for every Richard Branson or Stelios Haji-Iannou, who will crawl over broken glass to get a good profile in their chosen media, there are others who will dive for cover immediately they see a journalist come round the corner with notebook at the ready. This reticence is usually not too much of a problem for the person charged with getting the press coverage as long as there is support from the person at the top for the media campaign. If there isn't, of course, there probably won't be a media campaign anyway.

Nevertheless, it's useful for you to be able to deal with objections from lesser figures in the organisation in a tactful way, as and when they arise. There are a number of common objections and some standard ways of dealing with them:

Objection: it's a waste of my and my managers' time. You'll hear this one from managers who either have a narrow focus on their job or are under pressure. You can deal with the first objection by pointing out that media coverage is designed to help everybody in the organisation. Throw in a subtle hint that the person at the top – the managing director, chairperson or whoever is your sponsor in the media campaign – wants it to happen and will look favourably on those who help to facilitate good coverage. People with a narrow focus often also have a sharp sense of hierarchy. Knowledge that somebody "above" them in the organisation wants something to happen can change attitudes. Deal with the time pressure objection by pointing out that you're organising the media campaign so that most of the weight of doing it is removed from others onto your own broad shoulders. All you need is a few minutes of his or her time to collect some basic information. And, you'll add smiling sweetly, "if you're too busy to do it during office hours, I'm quite happy to stay on late to talk to you". It's surprising how often the individual concerned suddenly realises he or she has, after all, got a few moments to spare. Even if they do it with ill-grace.

Objection: this media relations is costing us too much. You'll generally hear this objection from somebody who takes a fairly jaundiced view of the media in general and who, in any case, ill understands the difference between press coverage and advertising. Advertising can be expensive and, yes, some of the money spent on it is wasted (as Lord Leverhulme famously pointed out). Press relations can be a remarkably cost-effective way of building media profile for the organisation. It's true that some organisations spend thousands of pounds a month hiring public relations consultancies. And it's also true that it's sometimes difficult to measure the benefit of that spend. But it's also possible to conduct a media campaign based on press releases at very low cost, especially if you are writing the releases yourself. You'll meet the cost objection by tactfully explaining the difference between advertising and media relations (if that is the root of the objection) then explaining what a cost-effective technique press releases can be.

Objection: media relations never worked before. This objection usually comes from people who either have a generally defeatist attitude to pretty much anything or who have seen media relations tried in the past and yield very little coverage. If somebody is one of life's natural defeatists, you won't be able to change their outlook on life. But you could win their (albeit grudging) co-operation with one of three ploys. First, you could point out that the boss has said it has to happen and, so, it has to happen. Defeatists are in awe of authority. Secondly, you could point out that the way in which the media relations was carried out in the past was flawed and you plan to do it a new way. This might win their help if there's even the chink of an open mind. Thirdly, you could bet them that the way you're planning to do it this time will generate, say, at least 50 column centimetres of coverage in newspapers and magazines within a month. They might feel obliged to take you on, if only to prove their point of view. Which means that, at least, they'll have to co-operate with you until you both know who's won the bet. (Set the coverage threshold low enough to make sure you're certain of trousering the winnings.)

Objection: the media wouldn't be interested in us. This objection comes from the individual who suffers from the corporate equivalent of low self-esteem. "Nobody wants to know about poor little me." The way to tackle this problem is to build confidence. You talk about all the positives in the organisation and point to the satisfied customers it has won or, if it's a voluntary organisation, the people it has helped. If the organisation has received letters from satisfied customers or thanks from people it has aided, you could use them as concrete evidence that there are people out there who think highly of it. If they think highly, why shouldn't others hear about the organisation's good work through the media. And, indeed, you can point out, case studies from satisfied customers or people who've been helped may even form a part of the media relations campaign. Besides, you'll add, the media certainly won't be interested in us if it never hears from us.

Objection: the media distorts everything anyway. So what's the point? your objector may add with a resigned shrug of the shoulders. There is no getting away from the fact that so-called "media distortion" is a problem for quite a number of people. That particularly applies to managers in those businesses who feel their company isn't being fairly portrayed. Sometimes, it also applies to voluntary organisations who believe that what they're seeking to achieve is inaccurately misrepresented. Of course, factual errors do occur in the media and, where they happen, they should be corrected. (We'll be looking at how to do this on page 146.) But the fundamental problem about media distortion often arises because of the way national red-top tabloids treat the news. A comparatively small number of organisations are going to be aiming much of their media relations at national red-top tabloids. The fact is that most newspapers, magazines and broadcast programmes do seek to be accurate and fair. At the same time, they are seeking to present "stories" and not just a collection of facts and, as a result, they usually shape information to present it in a way that serves the story they want to tell.

It is possible to be an unwitting victim of this story shaping process, but it is also possible in media relations to take steps to minimise its danger. (If you follow the 14-step approach, which starts on page 82, your organisation should be less vulnerable to misrepresentation.) You should discuss the "distortion" problem openly with your objector and describe the steps you're taking to minimise the danger of the organisation being misrepresented in the media. Besides, almost all business activities involve some risk – when you supply goods on credit, you can't always be one hundred per cent certain that you'll be paid – and doing media relations professionally means making the kind of effective risk assessment that should be undertaken for any kind of business activity, then taking steps to minimise those risks.

With your policy in place and objections bulldozed out of the way, you're ready to start looking for stories.

Chapter 5

Collecting information

The raw commodity that drives a media relations campaign is information. Without information, you have nothing to write about. Your first task as a press officer or publicist, therefore, is to get yourself organised so that you're in a position to get a steady flow of information that you can turn into press releases. Just how you set about this will, to some extent, depend on whether you are working in a large, medium or small organisation. It will also depend on whether you are working full-time as a press officer or combining the job with other duties.

Ways to find the facts

Let's start by looking at some of the issues involved in collecting information in three different sizes of organisation – large, medium and small.

Large organisation

If you're working in a large organisation, the chances are you're one of a team of people working on press and public relations. Perhaps you're part of a head office team or, maybe, you're working in one of the divisions or subsidiaries. If you're in the head office team, it's possible you may have a general oversight, but it's more likely that you'll be given the task of handling the company's media relations for a given range of products or services. In the public sector, you might be responsible for handling media relations for specific policy areas or services. Whichever position you're in, most of the general guidelines about collecting information will apply, but you'll need to be sensitive about straying into the areas covered by your colleagues. Sometimes, you may find that you need to co-operate with colleagues because the subject of your press release covers more than one area.

If you're working in a large organisation, you will also probably find that you're more likely to be involved in a major announcement of some kind – perhaps, for example, a significant new product launch or announcement of a new policy initiative in a public sector body. This kind of announcement often comes with a press pack which involves putting together a range of press releases that cover different aspects of the announcement. (We'll be dealing with putting together press packs on page 112.)

Finally, in a large organisation, you may well find there are more rules or standing orders about the kind of information that one person can pass to another as well as about the ways it should be done. You will need to be familiar with these rules and make sure you adhere to them.

Medium-sized organisation

In a medium-sized organisation, you may find that you're a full-time press officer but working with little or no dedicated staff support. You may be lucky enough to have a dedicated secretary or PA or you may find that you share one, perhaps with other people working in the marketing or sales function.

As a one-person band, you will need to be the kind of individual who's self-sufficient. You won't have the kind of large support infrastructure around you that your cousins in the large organisation have. At the same time, you won't have the kind of constraints about straying into other people's territory – the whole organisation is your informational oyster – and you probably won't have such restrictive rules about the handling of information.

As a result, you will need to become familiar with all the activities in your organisation and treat them all fairly when they're demanding your attention for the story that they want to get into the media. You may find there are more times when you're under pressure than large organisation press officers. Because you're a one-person band, there will be times when your office is unmanned. So you'll need to make arrangements for messages to be collected on voicemail or redirected to your mobile. If you're using voicemail, you need to check it regularly and get back to people who've called.

All this can be hard work, but if you have a self-sufficient personality, you could find being a press officer in a medium-sized organisation very satisfying.

Small organisation

If you're a press officer in a small organisation, you may be lucky enough to have a full-time post, but the chances are you have to double up your media duties with some other tasks. These could be on the marketing or sales side in the company or on the information or general administration side in a public sector organisation.

If you're a part-timer, you need to think carefully about how you plan to allocate your time between press relations and your other work. It may be that your manager has some clear ideas about this in which case the decision is made for you. But the problem when one person combines two or more jobs – given to them by one or more other people – is that the people giving the jobs tend to underestimate the amount of time they take. This is particularly true of press relations, especially when the manager in charge is unfamiliar with the activity. You may find you need to point out tactfully to your manager how much time you have in your week to devote to press relations activity and what you can reasonably achieve within that time.

One of the bugbears of being a part-timer is that you never seem to be around to collect information or take a call when the person you've been trying to get hold of is available. The danger here is that you could find it takes much longer to get the information you need for your press relations campaign simply because you can't get hold of the people you need when you're acting in press officer mode. The key to solving this problem is to plan ahead and become more adept at time management. If you think you're going to need information from an individual, plan to get it in plenty of time rather than leaving it to the last moment.

Although all this may sound rather frenetic, the upside of combining press relations with other duties is that you get plenty of variety in your work and this makes for an interesting life.

LOOKING FOR LEADS

Where on earth are you going to find information for press releases in your organisation? Of course, there are some organisations – large companies and central government departments, for instance – that have information bursting out all over. The problem you face if you work in an organisation where information is coming at you from all directions is how to filter and prioritise it. But that's a somewhat different issue.

For the moment, we want to concern ourselves with organisations which, on the face of it, don't have much to report to the media. On the face of it, being the operative qualification. Because, in truth, most organisations – large, medium and small – have stories to tell if only they know where to find them.

But press officers in many organisations face a double problem. One is finding stories that the media will be interested in. The other is fending off managers and others who have material that they would like to see in the press – but is never going to stand a chance of making it into print or onto the airwaves in a month of Sundays. There are times when you may need to be tactful and explain why the information you've been given will not be suitable for a press release. The best way to do that is to explain about the kind of information you do want – specifically, the kind of information the individual with the non-story might be able to provide.

Clearly, sources of information for press releases are going to vary widely depending on the size and nature of your organisation as well as the way information naturally flows around it. Perhaps you work in an organisation with an open culture where information is regularly made available to all. Perhaps you're employed by an organisation that takes a more restrictive view about who is entitled to know about what.

Whichever is the case, a good starting point in looking for news stories is to think about what might be the "news drivers" in your organisation. Sometimes that driver might be an individual, perhaps the person who leads the organisation. An obvious example from the commercial world is Richard Branson at Virgin. He is the organisation's principal news-maker and much of Virgin's press coverage revolves around what he says or does.

Alternatively, your main news driver may be your principal product. An example here is Microsoft's Windows operating system. A huge proportion of the press coverage devoted to the giant American software company is about its product which dominates the IT world. The main news driver could even be a regular event. The Royal Horticultural Society's Chelsea Flower Show receives a steady stream of coverage throughout the year as people prepare for the annual May event.

I've chosen examples from large or prominent organisations, but the same principle applies even if you're working in a small organisation, perhaps which operates only in one or two towns. Your chairman could still be a prominent local personality (or be made one by your press relations). Similarly, your products or the annual event you organise could be a key news driver.

It's important to bear in mind two other points. First, although it's useful to look for a main news driver and then focus on that, you shouldn't do so to the exclusion of other media opportunities. There are likely to be other things happening in your organisation which could make good copy. Secondly, your principal news driver might be something other than a person, a product or an event. And even if it isn't, there may also be other people, products and events – apart from the main news driver – that are worthy of news coverage.

Before we move on, there are two other sources of potential news stories that are worth mentioning. The first is the "place" story. You have a place story if you are doing something such as moving to a new office or opening a new branch. Such stories sometimes have an appeal for local media.

The other group of stories concerns a company's financial performance. If you are working in a public company, this will be of particular significance and there are detailed rules determining how financial information or other announcements that may have an impact on a company's share price can be released. For advice on this, you should consult the UK Listing Authority – details are

---

Ideas for press releases

People make news

People could make news when they:

Join your organisation

Retire

Are promoted or take on a new post

Are elected to a post in a professional or trade body

Win an award

Make a speech at a conference

Invent a new product

Take part in a charity event

Celebrate an important anniversary

Products make news

Products could make news when:

A new product is launched

Or re-launched in an improved version

Or a new product is acquired from another company

Or it takes a leading market share

Or is purchased by a well-know organisation

---

in appendix two on page 165.

If you work in a private company, you probably won't have any legal requirement to release financial information to the press, but you may want to do so if your company's financial record is good and underscores the growth and stability of the company.

Whatever your sources of information for press releases, you will need to develop good relationships with key contacts throughout the organisation. Getting good quality information for

Or is used by a celebrity

Or is exported for the first time

Or exported to a new country

Or the thousandth or millionth rolls off the production line

Or it is praised by independent analysts

Or new technology is used

Or new packaging is introduced.

Events make news

An event could make news when:

It's first announced

The first exhibitor/entrant signs up

Speakers/actors/bands are announced

Celebrity attendees are announced

New products on show are announced

A record number of advanced tickets have been sold

When it takes place

When a survey of attendees is published

When the next year's event is announced

use in media campaigns is largely a question of building trust with people who can provide it. If they know that the information will be used both wisely and effectively, they should become more and more willing to co-operate in your news gathering efforts as the organisation's media relations campaign develops.

But you will also need to develop the skill of extracting the information from them. One of the most common ways of doing this is through an interview.

Chapter 6

Conducting an interview

The problem with many press releases is that they go wrong right at the outset. And the outset is not when you start to write it, but when you start to collect the information. Too many releases simply don't contain all the information that's needed to satisfy an editor. So collecting information for the release is vitally important – and the most common way of collecting information is by conducting an interview.

Let's first clear away a few misconceptions about the kind of interviews you may need to conduct as a press officer or publicist. For a start, you can forget the kind of televisual interrogation that Jeremy Paxman or the like inflicts – the type that brings a mendacious politician out in a cold sweat. Television interviews of the confrontational type are designed as a form of theatre – the modern day equivalent of throwing Christians to the lions. They're done to entertain audiences and keep up viewing figures and, yes, hopefully to prise a new snippet of truth out of an important figure who'd prefer to keep inconvenient facts private.

Indeed, the word "interview" itself may be misleading in the context of collecting information for your press releases. Perhaps it would be better to call them conversations, because that word more captures the flavour of the type of interactions you'll be having with the people who provide you with information. Nevertheless, we'll stick to the word interview, because these are going to be conversations in which you ask most of the questions and your interlocutors provide most of the answers.

THREE INTERVIEW PRELIMINARIES

Before you conduct any interviews, there are three things you must do. Fail to do them and you'll create difficulties further down the track which may end up with you producing a substandard press release.

Understand your brief

The first of these is to understand the brief you've been given. This means understanding completely the subject of the release you've been asked to write and the target audience for it. Understanding the subject may seem a simple matter, but too often journalists receive press releases where it's simply not clear what the story is. Either the story is hidden away in a mass of background information of no particular interest or the release seems to contain two or more different stories each fighting for attention. (We'll be dealing with the question of writing the release clearly in chapter eight. For now, it is enough to flag up that you need to be aware of potential problems you may encounter at the writing stage before you conduct the interview.)

Understanding the target audience of the release is also important even before you start to collect information and conduct interviews. By target audience, I mean the readers of the publications or the viewers/listeners of the television or radio shows, to which you are going to send your release. Again, we'll be dealing with targeting in more detail in chapter seven which begins on page 69. For the time being, you should be aware of the kind of information your audience will want to know about – then make sure you collect it during your interviews.

Make contact with your interviewees

When you're asked to write a press release story, you may need to get the information from one or more people. In a simple story, it's likely that one person will have all the facts you'll need. In a complex story – or if you're writing a number of releases for a press pack to be used in a major announcement – you may have to speak to a number of people, perhaps scattered in offices around the country or even the world. The people you may need to speak to could include managers in your own organisation, customers, suppliers or other third-parties.

The purpose of this preliminary contact is so that you can get four initial bits of business out of the way. The first of these is to find out whether the individuals you're in touch with are happy to co-operate in the preparation of a press release. In the case of your own organisation, that will, hopefully, usually be the case. But it's by no means unheard of for turf wars to develop in organisations – one manager wanting to release information to the press, another to keep it under wraps. If you find yourself at the outset caught in one of these turf wars, you need to refer the matter to a manager who can resolve the dispute before you continue. But unless you have been given authority, don't favour one manager's view of the situation over another.

A more tricky situation arises when you are contacting people outside your organisation for help. A common situation is to be contacting customers in order to gain their co-operation for a case study or a "new order" press release. Over time, you will meet all kinds of reactions to this request, from those who want to rush round and help you draft the release to those who'll barely give you the time of day. It's important to try to keep a kind of detached composure whatever the reaction. A refusal can be frustrating but

excessive enthusiasm on the customer's part can create dangers
further down the track if it leads your press release into hyperbole
which can't be substantiated if a journalist chooses to dig deeper.
The best advice here is to make the request for help in a positive
but relatively low-key way and to stress that you are drafting a press
release from which you hope all parties mentioned will benefit.

The second bit of business in this contact-making phase is to
find a time when you can collect the information you need. Of
course, there will be instances where you've already got most of
the information you want from documents or other sources and
you only need to check a fact or two or, perhaps, get a quote. In
these cases, you can probably get the information you need simply
by calling or e-mailing the person who has it. But you may also
encounter situations where you need to collect more detailed
information or where you need to get facts or quotes from a
number of people. In these, it's useful to set up times when you
will conduct either a telephone or a face-to-face interview.

Another reason for operating this way is that much of the
information you get will be from people who lead busy lives. It's a
mistake to try to conduct an interview – even a short one – when
your interviewee has a dozen other things on his or her mind and
is just anxious to get you off the phone. You're more likely to get
the information if the person has had the chance to prepare and
has scheduled specific time to talk to you. With your own slot in
their diary, you've staked your own little place in their mindspace.

The third bit of business is to sort out with your interviewees
how you're going to conduct the interview. As we shall see (on
page 59), there are three main ways of conducting interviews –
face-to-face, by telephone or by e-mail. In most cases, it should
be possible to get the information you need by telephone. If you're

working in the same building as your interviewee, you may as well conduct the interview face-to-face, as it will take scarcely longer. However, you will sometimes encounter somebody who wants to have the interview face-to-face, even though you know you'd be able to get the information you need over the phone in about 10 minutes. Often, the reason for this is that they're a bit nervous about the interview and aren't sure whether they can give you the information you need. You can deal with this by reassuring them and pointing out that the interview is not necessarily a one-off exercise – you can check back if anything is unclear and, in any event, they'll be seeing a draft of the release before it's issued. On other occasions, they may want the interview face-to-face to satisfy their own sense of self-importance. In these instances, you may wish you could prick their balloon of pomposity, but if they have information you really need, you'll just have to make the journey, sit there, smile sweetly and ask your questions.

The fourth and final bit of business for this initial contact is to brief your potential interviewees on the ground you'll want to cover. You want the interview to run as smoothly as possible and to deliver the information you need. It is far more likely to do both if your interviewees know what's expected of them before it starts.

Think through your proposed interviews

When you've understood your brief and made contact with your interviewees, there is one more task to complete before you start on your interviews. That is to think through the structure of your interviews. Unless you really are just checking a couple of facts, you are likely to miss useful information if you don't go into each interview well prepared and knowing what you want to get out of it. You owe it to both yourself and your interviewees to get this

Sample notes for new product interview

Name of product?

When launched?

New or upgrade?

What does it do?

  • what's new here?

  • any major innovation?

  • what will users gain?

How positioned in market?

  • how different from competitors?

Who will be main users?

  • any already?

How large estimated market?

  • any research here?

What about distribution channels?

  • special offers?

  • maintenance and support?

  • wholesale and retail price?

Marketing and promotion?

Who's heading the launch?

Technical detail for background?

right. Although you have briefed your interviewees on what you want from them, to a large extent they will be relying on you to prompt them to give the information during the interview.

You probably don't want to write out your questions word for word – and you won't get the best effect by doing so. It will give your interview an over-controlled regimented feel in which the interviewee may feel too constrained by your formal manner to

---

Sample notes for new branch opening interview

Branch name?

Address of branch?

How large?

- number of staff?
- recruiting?
- square feet?

Size of investment in branch?

What will happen there?

What territory covered?

How will it benefit the area?

When opening?

-       • any ceremony?

Any special activities at branch?

Why this branch now?

Name of manager/head?

- brief biographical details?

---

speak freely. But you could certainly make a series of simple notes covering the main points you want covered. There are two examples of how you can set out your notes on this and the previous page.

When you are collecting information for press releases, the six most important words which you should always keep in mind are who, what, when, where, why – and how. Whatever the topic, if your press release fails to answer these basic questions, it's likely to frustrate or annoy those who receive it. So:

Who are the main players in the story?

What are they doing?

When did they do it or will be doing it?

Where did they do it?

Why did they do it?

How did they do it?

As a way of keeping these important words in mind, why not memorise Rudyard Kipling's rhyme:

I keep six honest serving men

(They taught me all I knew);

Their names are What and Why and When

And How and Where and Who. (*The Elephant's Child*, 1902)

THREE WAYS TO CONDUCT AN INTERVIEW

As we have seen, there are three main ways in which you can conduct your interviews – face-to-face, over the telephone or by e-mail. You need to consider which is the most appropriate in each case.

Face-to-face

You could need to do a face-to-face interview for a number of reasons. The first is that you need to collect a large amount of information. In years of interviewing as a journalist, I've worked on the rule of thumb that if an interview is likely to last more than about three-quarters of an hour, it's best to do it face-to-face. It's simply difficult to sustain a high-energy conversation over the telephone for much more than that time.

The second reason is that you might need to review complex papers, see equipment or look round a building or other facility of some kind as part of the interviewing process. Of course, there are cases when doing these things is important and seeing with your own eyes enables you to write with more insight about the subject. In my experience, however, the interviewee is more likely to believe you need to see at first hand than is actually the case. This is because the interviewee is rarely aware of the "weight" of the story you're writing and the amount of information you need. Obviously, you need to judge each case on its merits, but my experience certainly suggests that when it comes to conducting interviews, a lot of time-consuming and costly travel takes place unnecessarily.

A third reason for conducting a face-to-facer is when you have an interviewee who is too clammed up to be interviewed over the telephone or who insists on it. You can certainly get more out of people when you're looking them in the eye. But as a press release writer, you won't be searching for the uncomfortable revelations that eager journalists are after. (Well, perhaps you'll be seeking them, but you won't be allowed to use them in your releases.)

And the final reason for choosing face-to-face is that it's simply sensible to do so because the person you need to interview is close at hand, perhaps in the same building – maybe even in the same room.

Telephone

The telephone is ideal for shorter interviews. I said earlier that, for interviews longer than three-quarters of an hour, you should be thinking of face-to-face but, in my experience, the best telephone interviews seem to run out at between 20 minutes and half an hour. Most busy people are happy to consider a telephone interview if only because it doesn't sound quite so formal and it doesn't threaten to take up so much of their valuable time.

It is now simple to record telephone conversations which means that you can conduct an interview and then transcribe the tape afterwards. Recording a telephone interview means you can collect quite a lot of detailed information in a reasonably short time. (See appendix two on page 165 for a company that supplies telephone conversation recording equipment.) If you are planning to record a telephone interview, make sure that you tell your interviewee before you ask your first question. In fact, it is a useful courtesy to mention that you will be recording the interview when you set up the appointment.

E-mail

In a few cases, you may want to conduct an interview by e-mail. This is not ideal for detailed or complex interviews, but there are some circumstances where it can come into its own.

The first of these is when you are trying to interview somebody overseas in a different time zone. If it's difficult to fix a time when you're both at the end of a telephone, then it's worth suggesting e-mail. A second reason is when your interviewee wants to provide some technical or complex information in his or her own words. A variation on this is where you simply need to get a couple of quotes to spike your story. It can be much quicker getting these over e-mail than by telephone.

The key to successful e-mail interviewing is to pose your questions in a very precise way so that it is clear to your interviewee what information you are seeking. On those occasions when I've used this approach, I've sometimes posed a question and then added some extra detail in brackets after it about the kind of information that might be included in the answer.

There is an e-mail option which I've never used myself but which seems perfectly practical. That is to conduct an interview using MSN Messenger. Using it, you are able to develop an interactive approach with your interviewee and follow-up on questions which you feel haven't been fully answered. However if you are both sitting in front of PCs tapping out questions and answers on MSN Messenger, there doesn't seem to be any reason why you can't be talking on the telephone.

Interviews: where and how

Two issues you need to consider even before you've asked your first question are where you're going to conduct the interview and how. The where concerns the physical location of the interview and the how is all about whether you're going to take notes or tape record the interview

Finding the right place

If you're conducting a face-to-face interview, finding a good place for it is important. That's true whether you plan to take notes or to tape-record the interview. Essentially, you need a location where both you and your interviewee feel comfortable. In most cases, interviewees feel comfortable in their own office or a meeting room at their offices. Home turf seems to give them an extra aura of confidence they may lack if they've had to find their way to an unfamiliar location.

However, wherever they are, it is usually important to find a room where you can be alone with your interviewee. Of course, it's not impossible to conduct an interview in an open-plan office, but if it's a busy office, then the level of distractions could be annoying both to you and your interviewee.

If you're meeting away from your interviewee's office, you may well find yourself conducting the interview in a hotel or at an exhibition. In my experience, neither are ideal locations for a longish interview. But if there's no alternative try to find a quiet spot, such as a private room. Certainly, try to find somewhere where there won't be a large number of people passing by or where there is a lot of background noise.

Location can also be important when you're conducting a telephone interview. Many people do work in open-plan offices and they don't like colleagues earwigging them while they're doing an interview. Suggest to your interviewee that he or she might like to find a private office for the interview. Finally – and this is a personal point – I dislike speaker phones. The sound is usually distorted and that can prove a problem if the interviewee doesn't possess a very clear speaking voice or has a thick accent. It can be embarrassing constantly asking somebody to repeat something. Try to persuade your interviewee to pick up the handset!

Noting or recording

Before you conduct your interview you'll need to decide whether you plan to take notes or record it. There are pros and cons in both cases.

Taking notes is probably the best way if you're a speedy note-taker with shorthand at 100 words a minute. But, let's face it, who of us are? No offence, but it's quite likely your shorthand or speedwriting speed isn't fast enough to record verbatim what your interviewee says. It's entirely possible, of course, that you don't need a verbatim transcript of what's said – merely a record of key points. In which case your shorthand or speedwriting may be equal to the task. Even so, there is something of a skill to talking and note-taking at the same time. And, from my experience, it's more difficult to develop a really good conversation with somebody when you're busy taking notes. It's as though the notebook gets in the way. But, if you do take notes, at least you have the information you need ready to write up as soon as you get back to your PC.

That is not the case if you tape-record the interview. Recorders are now small and light enough to slip into a pocket or handbag. They come in versions which record either on tapes or on a computer chip. In the case of the former, you need a transcription unit which enables you to control with a foot-pedal the speed at which you listen to the tape. In the case of the latter, you download a file of your interview on to your PC, then use a special piece of software to transcribe the interview using a foot-pedal to control the speed.

The big advantage of recording interviews is that you don't, in theory, miss anything because you can listen to them again and again. But, in fact, you do occasionally miss things if you haven't recorded clearly. It can sometimes be irritating to have to go back and check names or technical terms which you can't hear clearly on the tape. Transcribing recordings can prove an irritating chore but it does, at least, enable you to listen slowly to the interview again – so you may pick up points that you'd missed.

Interviews: getting the best results

Interviewees range from the laid-back and endlessly garrulous to the up-tight and monosyllabic. Whatever your interviewees are like, you will get more out of them if you adopt a relaxed approach to the interview.

Set the tone right at the outset by seeking to put your interviewee at ease with a few commonplace remarks. The key is to get them talking to you – about the weather, the latest football results or anything. Stimulating a two-way flow of words is an excellent ice-breaker. I've found it pays to spend a few moments putting an interviewee at ease in a telephone interview but that you can often sense when he or she wants to get down to the business in hand. In the case of a face-to-face interview, you'll probably spend a little longer in idle chit-chat before switching on your recorder or getting out your notebook.

The best way to conduct an interview is to start at the beginning and work your way through. Deal with the events or topics you want to talk about chronologically. Often your interviewee won't really have a good idea of where the beginning is or the order in which you want the information, so it's important that you seek in a gently low-key way to impose your structure on the interview right at the outset.

Try to prevent your interviewee leaping from one subject to another. And don't be afraid to ask the same question in a different form of words if you feel you didn't get the information you wanted in the first answer. I find it's useful to let a subject talk for a bit and, when they reach a natural pause, come back to two or three points they mentioned about which I need further information before moving on to the next topic. Even if you're recording an interview, it can be useful to jot one or two word *aide memoires* on your interview plan to remind you of the points you want to explore more deeply.

If you find your interviewee is going off at a tangent or descending into too much detail, it's quite acceptable to interject as he or she takes breath and say something like: "What I really meant by my question was…" The key is to keep your subject focused on the information you want to get. In doing this, you also need to keep in mind three points.

The first is that some of your subjects may have a "presumption of understanding". They may think you know more about the topic than you do. If you're not an expert, it's usually a good idea to make this clear at the outset. Often, interviewees are only too delighted to find they're being interviewed by a neophyte in their subject because it's a great opportunity to show off their depth of understanding. But the key point you have to bear in mind, whether you understand what your interviewee is talking about or not, is whether the readers of the release will understand it. You need to get the story in terms that they will want to read.

The second point you should remember is that news stories work best when they've got plenty of facts in them. Your press release is likely to be a news story of sorts and so you should make sure you're collecting the facts you need to write a tight story that will look to a journalist as though it "stands up" – that is, it has all the facts to justify and support the story's central thesis. For now, it is enough to note that you need to get the facts and you need to get them right.

The third point is the need to keep the mutual back-slapping and self-promotion under control. When you're collecting information for press releases, it's natural that your subjects will be enthusiastic about their new company, product, branch, event or cause. But the readers of stories about it will principally want to know what it is rather than how great you or your interviewee think it is. One of the greatest faults with most press releases is that the self-flattery is laid on thickly with a palette-knife. It is, arguably, the greatest single factor which turns off journalists about press releases and it may kill a perfectly good story. Avoiding this fundamental error starts when you are collecting information for your release – stick to the facts, not the flattery.

How will you know when you've got enough information from the interview? The simple answer is when you're confident you've

Ten tips for great interviews

1   Prepare in advance
2   Arrive on time
3   Inspire confidence through your appearance
     and voice
4   Know what you want from the interview
5   Check facts, especially names, figures, etc
6   Tease out interesting detail
7   Say when you don't understand something
8   Be politely persistent in getting the facts
     you need
9   Check back afterwards for any facts you missed
10   Thank the interviewee for his or her help – you may
     need it again

covered all the points in your interview plan in sufficient detail. But before you bring an interview to a conclusion, you might also want to do a quick mental check to ensure that key points have been covered, that you have all the name spellings checked and that any doubtful facts or figures have been double checked. It's important to have an end point in view because there are some interviewees who like to talk for ever! All you need to do is to say that you now think you've got enough information for your press release and thank your subject for his or her time. Closing your notebook decisively or turning off your recorder is a good way to signal that the interview is over. But before you leave or put down the phone, make sure you have your subject's contact details and permission to call back if you need to check anything.

After the interview

The interview hasn't ended when you've put down the telephone or left your interviewee's office. It's a little bit too easy to look on completing an interview as an end in itself – especially a big interview that's required a lot of preparation. But the job isn't finished until you've written your press release. So, assuming that you've completed all your interviews and collected all the other information you need, write your story as soon as possible.

It's not just that the facts will be fresh in your mind – which is worth more than having them down in a set of notes – it's that you'll still have the original enthusiasm for the story which, hopefully, the interviews helped to stimulate. Moreover, because you will need to get approval for your release, the sooner you can send a draft to those people you've interviewed who need to see it, the more you're likely to impress them with your efficiency. You'll get them to respond more quickly with any comments or necessary approvals because quick turnarounds tend to generate a sense of urgency.

CHAPTER 7

FINDING MEDIA TARGETS

If you're new to the business of press release writing, asking who you should be sending a press release to before you've even written it may sound like putting the cart before the horse. Sadly for journalists, it seems that quite a few experienced press release writers also only decide on their distribution lists after they've written the release. They adopt the scattergun rather than the laser gun approach to press release distribution.

But targeting is one of the keys to success when you're trying to get your press release published. And you cannot hope to write a release that satisfies your target publications, or radio or tv programmes, if you don't know what they are before you start tapping away at your PC. If you have a clear understanding of your targets, then you are in a much better position to craft a release that will make them sit up and take notice.

You may think, so what? Does it really matter if a few journalists who aren't interested get the release as long as it hits the ones that are? If the number of releases that miss their target by a mile is anything to go by, there are quite a few press officers and publicists who think this way. But it's dangerous thinking which has a long-term corrosive effect on the view journalists take of all press releases.

THREE REASONS TO TARGET

There are three problems about the scattergun approach to distributing press releases which you should seek to avoid.

The first is what I call the "irritant factor". Author, playwright and newspaper columnist Keith Waterhouse summed this up very well when he wrote: "Ninety-five per cent of the handouts that reach me as a Daily Mail columnist don't even reach the scrunching stage. They glide unread and often unopened – you get to recognise the envelopes – straight from desk to bin." You can tell what Waterhouse thinks about press releases by his use of the word "handouts", a term more commonly associated with dole queues and soup kitchens. Quite simply, irritating journalists when you don't have anything relevant to provide, is not good preparation for approaching them when you do have a hot story.

The second point is that you waste money spending time preparing and sending releases to journalists who are never going to use them. If you value your time, you should be spending it developing and targeting story ideas that will be of interest to journalists. Many releases are distributed by e-mail at little direct cost, but there are still thousands sent out the conventional way through the post achieving little more than providing revenue for the Royal Mail.

There is a final reason why you need to understand your targets before you write your release. One of the problems I've noticed with press releases is an attempt by the authors to provide something for everybody. It's almost as though they know even before they've started to write that they must try and provide a focus of interest for every journalist from the reporter on the local paper, through specialist columnists on trade and technical mags, to section editors on nationals. But by trying to provide something for everybody, they end up satisfying nobody. The release lacks a clear point. The story – if there is one – gets lost in a muddle of confusing information. The problem could have been avoided by developing one clear focus at the outset, then crafting a release designed to satisfy it and no other.

IDENTIFYING YOUR PRIME AUDIENCE

Before you even start writing press releases, ask yourself this question: who is your prime audience? In other words, which group or groups of people do you really want to be reading your messages in the press or hearing them on the radio or tv? (There are some examples of audiences on page 74.) Unless you can answer this question with a reasonable degree of precision, your media campaign is likely to miss the target.

Yet these can prove to be surprisingly difficult questions to answer. The reason is that most organisations have more than one focus for their activities. Sometimes their audiences can be remarkably diverse. Because you think that what your organisation is doing is important, it's very easy to slip into a mindset that believes everybody else must also think it's important. The fact is: they won't.

Nevertheless, many organisations – even quite small ones – may have multiple audiences. The danger is trying to satisfy all these audiences at the same time. It's not usually possible for two key reasons. The first is that each part of your audience may be interested in different aspects of your message. Customers, for example, may be interested in what your new product can do to aid their business. Suppliers will be more interested in whether there are any opportunities to supply parts or components for your new product.

The second reason is that you may need to reach different parts of your audience through different media. For example, a large store chain selling, among other products, high fashion, good food and fine wines may want to reach fashionistas through Glamwear Monthly, gourmets through The Foodie and tipplers through Wine Snob Weekly. This is a very obvious example. The problem you may face is that it's more difficult to differentiate your audiences.

The first step in doing this well is to go back to the market segmentation exercise your company should already have carried out when it developed its marketing strategy. (Even if you're a public sector or voluntary organisation, it may still be useful to apply the principles of market segmentation.) Getting a clear idea about the markets you're seeking to sell to (or the publics you want to provide services for) is an essential first step in any press relations campaign.

The segmentation exercise may well throw up a number of possible targets. They won't all be equally important. In order to develop a sensible strategy for your press relations campaign, you need to have a clearer idea of which are the prime targets and which are secondary. It's useful to think of the targets being clustered around a bullseye. One or two – the most critical – will fall on the bullseye itself. Others will be closer, some farther out. Looking at the picture you've created provides an excellent visual representation of your campaign priorities.

How to get a journalist in your sights

When you are clear about who your key target audiences are, you next need to think about how you're best going to reach them. There are plenty of sources of information about newspapers and magazines – as well as the journalists who write for them – about radio and television programmes and about websites which may be interested in your releases. These sources (which we'll come to shortly) have a varying level of detail, accuracy – and cost.

But if my experience is anything to go by – and from talking to fellow journalists, I know that it is – many if not most PR people ignore the most valuable source of information of all, the magazines and newspapers themselves. It's quite clear from the way press releases are sprayed out indiscriminately that, in some cases, the press officers sending them have never set eyes on a single copy of the publication which is their unlucky recipient. (The same applies to many of the PR people who ring up to offer story ideas to journalists. It's plain within seconds of the conversation starting that the PR hasn't bothered to get hold of a copy of the publication in question before lifting the telephone. If you're guilty of this professional solecism consider this: it's not only a pretty inefficient way of placing your story, but a bit of an insult to the editor to admit that you haven't even bothered to glance at his publication before calling with the story he simply can't refuse.)

But, perhaps, that's an argument for another day. For the moment, let's concentrate on targeting journalists. There is really no substitute for building your own database of relevant journalists. In some cases, the word "database" may aggrandise what may be details about just a handful of journalists. For example, if you're a local organisation operating in only one small town, there are unlikely to be more than a couple of newspapers and, perhaps, a radio station that are likely to be interested in your activities. If you're a multinational company, you're at the other end of the spectrum and you could be talking about hundreds or even thousands of potential media contacts. The vast bulk of organisations will find themselves falling between those two ends of a very broad spectrum.

Audience appreciation

Depending on your organisation, you may want to reach several of the following audiences:

Customers
The most obvious, but you may want to segment further if you have a range of products appealing to different classes of customer.

Previous customers
Often overlooked, but some marketers say they are the most fruitful audience from which to recruit new business.

Rival's customers
These will, presumably, be similar kinds of people to those who buy your own products. But don't assume they will be exactly the same if your rival's company positions itself differently – perhaps up or down market.

Possible users
People who could use your product or service but don't consider themselves potential customers because they don't know about your product or even your company – or even realise that it may be relevant to their needs.

Dealers/distributors
Companies that could be selling your product or service. They'll need different kinds of messages to end-users of the product.

Retailers
Shops who could be selling your product – they may

need messages that differ from those used with dealers or distributors.

Suppliers

Even though they rely on you for business, don't underestimate the added value you can gain from building a more positive image with them.

Local communities

Especially important if what you do has a significant impact on local people in the area where your premises are based.

Policy makers

Especially those who make policies that can have an impact on your business. They may exist at local, regional, national, European or international level – or, depending on the nature of your business, all of them.

Investors

A vital audience if you're a public company, but also important for private companies that may want to raise funds from institutions or individuals such as "business angels".

Regulators

Many businesses are now regulated in some way. It pays to create a positive climate in which the detailed scrutiny your business receives from regulators takes place.

Advocacy groups

Increasingly important as businesses can come under pressure from bodies with mandates to campaign on a wide range of issues.

Whether you find yourself falling towards the lower end, the higher end or somewhere in the middle will determine how you decide to compile and store the information you hold about journalists. If you have only a few names, perhaps no more than a dozen or 20, it might be simplest to store the information on a card file. If you start to move above 20, certainly above 50, you ought to consider compiling your own computerised database of press contacts.

But whichever method you use to compile and store the information, the reasons for doing so are the same. First, the commercial sources of information you can access (at a cost) about publications and journalists provide a valuable baseline of information. But depending on the frequency with which they are compiled and edited, they will always be out of date – slightly or perhaps significantly. Perhaps slightly out of date doesn't matter too much for some of your marginal contacts. It matters a lot for those targets at the centre of your media bullseye.

The second point is that the commercial lists contain varying levels of detail about publications and journalists. By compiling your own database, you have the opportunity to add that extra detail about specific issues and stories which tend to crop up in particular publications, or the special interests of individual journalists, which enables you to target your releases with the kind of laser beam precision that gets much better results. Knowing more about target publications also helps you to spot publicity opportunities which others may have overlooked.

There is a military adage: time spent on reconnaissance is rarely wasted. The same applies to the world of writing and sending press releases. So where can you find the information you need?

SOURCES OF TARGETING INFORMATION

In fact, PR people are spoilt for choice, but most information sources have their advantages and disadvantages.

Benn's Media

Let's start with the grand-daddy of them all, Benn's Media directories, first published in 1846. Nowadays, these are an impressive set of four volumes containing listings of media. Volume one covers the United Kingdom, volume two the rest of Europe, volume three North America, and volume four most of the rest of the world. In all, the four volumes pack in 78,000 media entries with 187,500 named contacts in 214 countries. Individual volumes cost (in 2005) £192 with a special offer of £395 for all four. Benn's isn't a bad place to start if you want a low-cost and easy first port of call. The downside is that, like all printed directories, it is slightly out of date even by the time it is published and becomes progressively more out of date as time passes. Details from www.cmpdata.co.uk

Willings Press Guide

An alternative (or, possibly, even an addition) to Benn's is Willings Press Guide, also a long-established directory. This comes in three volumes covering, respectively, the UK, Western Europe and the World (excluding those countries covered in the first two volumes). The Guide provides information on 65,000 publications and media outlets which makes its range somewhat smaller than Benn's. However, unlike Benn's, there is also an online version, Willings Online, which is updated every three months. This makes searching easier and even lets you produce name and address labels in PDF format. The 2005 cost for Willings' service was £375 plus VAT. Details: www.romeike.com.

Editors

Editors media directories have been around since 1982 and provide a very comprehensive listing of who's who and what's what in the British media. They also handily come in six compact volumes which means you don't find your arms yanked out of your sockets when you pick them up. Overall, there are 50,000 named editorial contacts on 15,000 publications and radio and television stations as well as specific programmes. But, as with any printed volume, expect some of the names you're contacting to have moved on by the time you come to use the directory. Even so, if you're likely to want to use a wide range of media at different times, these directories could prove useful. Volume one covers national and Sunday papers together with news agencies and radio and tv. Volume two deals with business and professional publications, volume three with regional newspapers and tour guides, volume four with consumer and leisure magazines and volume five with television and radio programmes. Volume six is a useful round-up of freelancers together with members of the Writers' Guild (which represents writers in TV, film, radio, theatre, animation and books). And, at the time of writing, a seventh volume on internet media was due out. The downside is that the individual volume prices (2005) at £299, except for volume six at £225, are on the pricey side. But all six volumes are available for £675 and no doubt there will be a deal for all seven. Details: www.romeike.com

PR Planner

If you want something a bit more sophisticated than a printed directory – even one that's updated online – you might want to consider PR Planner which has appeared for years on CD-Rom and is now coming out on DVD. It lets you search for publications and journalists on your PC screen and compile press lists which you can then print straight on to labels. Alternatively, you can produce e-mail or fax lists for distribution (but be aware that most journalists don't take kindly to you distributing your press releases on their fax paper). The disk contains 120,000 contacts in 49,000 organisations in the UK and the rest of Europe and it's updated every quarter so you can be reasonably certain you're working with contemporary information. The 2005 price of the DVD with UK-only information was £875 plus VAT. Details: www.romeike.com.

Mediadisk

If Benn's Directory is the grand-daddy of press contact services, Mediadisk is the big daddy of them. It is, essentially, an online database service with 700,000 contacts – a number that is larger than the population of 39 countries – in more than 165,000 media outlets around the world. This is clearly a service for the big user not least because it's the highest-tech of the services on offer. Romeike, which operates the service, says that Mediadisk receives about 2,000 updates a day which sounds good until you realise that means each of the 700,000 entries is only updated on average about once a year. Not all entries would need updating annually but some would need more frequent updates. Mediadisk has two helpful features. One is the ability to look up forward article plans on newspapers and magazines rather than trawling through other sources. The other is the ability to record activities and correspondence with individual journalists using the relationship management part of the system. But all this comes at a price. In 2005, a single-user licence for UK and Eire data cost £3,108 plus VAT. Details: www.romeike.com

A question of timing

Before we leave the question of targeting press releases and move on to writing them, we need to consider the key issue of timing. Not a few press releases miss the mark simply because they turn up at the wrong time. So timing ought to be an essential part of your targeting strategy.

Subjects which make regular features or supplements

Accountancy

Architecture

Books

Careers

Commercial property

Cooking

Eating out

Education

Films

Gardening

Health

Media

Motoring

Music

Personal finance

Property

Social work

Theatre

Travel

Women's interests

If you pick up a week's copies of practically any national or regional daily newspaper, you will see that they have a regular pattern of covering certain specialist subjects on particular days. Of course, mainstream national and international, business and sports news are in the paper every day. But most dailies at both national and regional level carry columns, pages or whole supplements on special subjects at least one day a week. A listing of some of these subjects is in the panel on page 80.

In the national and regional press, there are some fairly common themes. Property, for example, tends to appear on Wednesday or Thursday because home buyers are thinking of looking round for a house at the weekend. The same reasoning applies to motoring specials which often appear on Thursday or Friday. In fact, activities which involve people using their leisure time, such as gardening, reading books or going to the cinema, are likely to be dealt with in papers towards the end of the week. On the other hand, specialised subjects to do with people's work, such as education, social work, law, accountancy and the media itself tend to get dealt with earlier in the week.

The obvious point – which, unfortunately, doesn't seem to be obvious to all PR practitioners – is to submit your release in time to meet the relevant deadline. That may be relatively straightforward if you're dealing with a paper that runs a column or page in the main paper. If you're dealing with a special supplement, you may find that there is more than one deadline – perhaps for features and news pages.

Having identified the right place, it would be a crying shame to miss out by sending your release at the wrong time and lose the opportunity to get some helpful coverage.

Chapter 8

Build a press release in 14 steps

When you set out to draft a press release, the first thing you have to write is the headline. Right?

Wrong. It's one of many myths which seem to circulate about press release writing and also just one (among many) of the reasons why such a high proportion of releases fail to hit the spot with journalists. What follows in this chapter is a 14-step approach which should put you on the right tracks to drafting a basic release. (In the next chapter, we'll look at some extra techniques you can use to give your release added editor appeal.)

Step 1: Know the point of your story

Journalists often receive press releases which are a mish-mash of confusing information with no discernible point. Sometimes this will be the result of a press officer being asked to put out a release by some high-up in the organisation in order to "get us in the papers". On other occasions, it will be because the release is the result of a joint exercise in which everybody, including the office cat, has made their contribution. The simple rule here is that if you don't know what the point of your story is, you shouldn't be issuing a press release.

But it's not so simple. Many press officers think they know what the point of their release is, but in fact they've missed it. The missed point comes in many guises. The company reports its annual profits are £100,000. Boring. The missed point was that the company had made a profit the year after it had been rescued from liquidation by a new management team. First prize for vegetables at the village produce show was won by Joan Smith. Boring. First prize at the show was won by Joan Smith, a spina bifida sufferer who does all her gardening from a wheelchair.

Sometimes the missed point occurs because the press officer doesn't have a sharp enough "nose" for news – as in the case of the turnaround company. Sometimes it may be through a mistaken belief that telling the true story will cause offence, as in the case of Joan Smith. On still other occasions, the press officer has got the point, but internal politics has watered it down so that a robust soup of a story has turned into a thin gruel.

Another problem is mixing several stories together so that it's not clear what the main point is as in a story that starts something like this:

Charlie Farnsbarn has been appointed managing director of Moneymaking Financial Advisers, which has announced record profits, is moving offices and launching a new range of insurance plans.

No doubt the writer will try and sort out all these themes later in the release, but it might be better to save them for three shorter and simpler releases issued at different times. In summary, the point of your release is the point. Search for the sharpest news hook before you even start to write your release.

Step 2: Check your story passes the "so-what?" test

You may have defined with commendable precision the point of your story – you have your news hook – but when editors receive your press release will they care? Journalists are sometimes portrayed – not entirely without justification – as a cynical bunch. Partly, this is because they're fed a whole lot of misleading information and half-truths by people who should know better but are more interested in defending their interests by deception. But, partly, it's because they're on the receiving end of a torrent of information which they know won't be of any conceivable interest to their readers.

You can apply the same "so-what?" test that journalists use when they see a press release: what would we be missing if we didn't carry this story? If you can't show that they would be missing something useful, you haven't got a story that will interest them. But let's enter a caveat here. Each journalist will apply the so-what? test differently – for example, a writer on a national newspaper will take a different view from the editor of a technical journal. What you have to do is to make sure that your release passes the so-what? test of each and every journalist you send it to.

Step 3: Assemble all needed information

Another big fault with press releases is that they lack all the information they need to make the story stand up. This problem presents itself in a number of guises. A company has signed its largest contract yet, but we don't know the value. The chairman of the Rotary Club has been presented with a long-service award, but we don't know how many years he's been with the club. The company has launched a new version of its product, but we don't know what the key difference is from the previous version.

When you write a press release you should be answering questions, not leaving them hanging in the air. So it's important to make sure that you've got all the information you need before you start to write. Ask yourself whether you're lacking vital facts that a journalist would need to complete the story. That includes important detail such as people's job titles, product names and office locations – any fact whose absence would render the story incomplete.

But there's more to gathering information than that. Speak to journalists and they'll tell you that a particularly irritating type of press release is the one that looks as though it has a story until you start to dig deeper. The fact is that some press release stories simply disintegrate when they're poked by an even half-probing journalist. A typical example is the "survey" story. An organisation purports to have discovered sensational findings from an in-depth survey. It turns out that the survey questioned half a dozen people and the writer's parrot. A company is thrilled to announce a big name new user for its product. It turns out the big name has been using the product for months (or even, in some cases, years) and has only just given permission for its name to be used. So it is not a "new" user at all.

The lesson here is that you must have all the information you need to support the story you want to tell. That includes not only the information you'll use in the release but additional information journalists may ask for in order to flesh out the angle they want to put on their story. Fail to do this and you risk getting a reputation as somebody who issues unreliable stories – the kiss of death as far as future coverage is concerned.

Step 4: Judge the weight of your story

How important is your story? To you, it's probably very important. But that's not the point. The real question you should be asking is: how important is this story likely to be for the journalists who will receive it? At a basic level, this is what's involved in judging the weight of a story. Quite simply, how much coverage is it likely to get? Will it make the front page? An inside page lead? A second or third story on a page? Or merely a "nib" – an in-brief item of a paragraph or two?

Press officers who can judge the weight of their story are more likely to get more of their releases used. This is partly because they will have then written the story to an appropriate length. Writing to length forces you to select the most important information. If you're writing a story with weight, you might want to write two or, at most, three pages of double-spaced text. At this length, you have room to include plenty of detail and some quotes from two or three players in the story.

If you're writing to one page length, then you have to be much more selective about your facts. You must be certain to include only the really important facts, but at the same time give the story enough context (see step seven) to make its significance obvious to the journalists who will read it. If you know in your heart of hearts that your story is never going to make more than a nib, then write it as a nib of two or three paragraphs. (If journalists decide to upgrade the story, they'll soon get back to you for more information.)

There are two very powerful reasons why you should judge the weight of your story and write it to length. The first is that you're showing the journalists you send it to that you have a realistic view of the importance of the story. You're acting like a professional. Because they only want a limited amount of copy about the story, they don't need to wade through pages of irrelevant detail to find what they want. The second reason is that by writing to length and giving only the most important facts – the material you really want to see in print – you make it more likely that that is what will be used. The journalist simply doesn't have the option of digging through a mass of other information. You've raised the odds of seeing the facts you consider important – rather than some marginal information – in print.

Step 5: Focus on your target audience

We have already looked in depth at why it's important to understand your target audience (see page 69). But now, as you sit poised in front of your keyboard, is the time to make another mental check that you're entirely clear in your own mind whom you're writing for.

There are two reasons why it's essential to focus, focus, focus as you write. First, because it will influence the choice of facts you select to use in your story. Consider a company that's just won an important industry award. The unfocused press officer will send the same release to the trade press and to the local newspapers in the town where the organisation has its offices. But each of these will be looking for different facts. The trade press will want to know about the business innovation or technical processes which helped to win the award. The local press will be more interested in local people who played a part in the triumph or who collected the award at the presentation.

The second reason why you need to focus, focus, focus as you tap away at the keys is that the audience you're writing for determines the language you should use. In the example of the award winning company, you could comfortably employ commonly used industry terms and acronyms in your release knowing that both journalists and their readers would understand them. If you needed to use a technical term in the local press release, you'd have to explain it – if you couldn't avoid using it altogether.

So don't underestimate the power of focus to make your press release really do its job.

Step 6: Write the introduction

At last! You're ready to write the first sentence of your press release. And the first sentence of your press release should contain the story. Nothing else. Just the story. No background information about your company's markets, inflated claims about its products or skills, potted history of its triumphs, or thoughtful insights into its finances and ownership. Just the story.

Trouble is, very few press releases do contain the story in the first sentence. And even if they do, it will as likely as not be camouflaged by a mass of other verbiage. The simple rule is this: when you're clear in your mind what your story is, try to explain the most important point about it in simple language in the first sentence. Exclude all information which doesn't support the main point unless it is absolutely vital to understanding that point. As you write your intro (and, indeed, the rest of the copy) don't assume the journalist reading it will have the kind of detailed insight about it you've acquired as a result of your researches.

You can find out how to write effective press release intros partly by avoiding the elephant traps which 98 per cent of press releases fall into. The most common ones are:

Trap 1: the story-teller. It's true that, in media terms, you're writing a story but you're not a story-teller. In other words, you don't start at the beginning and work your way through to the end in a chronological narrative. You should go straight to the most important point first. So, for example, a story concerning a fashion designer who is about to show her first West End collection shouldn't start: "Maria Furbelow was only 14 when she first saw her mother sewing on buttons and decided she wanted to become a dress designer." It should get straight to the point: "Maria Furbelow will show her first autumn collection at the Bond Street Gallery next Tuesday." The fact she was inspired to become a dress designer by watching her old Mum sew on buttons can come further down the story.

Trap 2: background briefing. Too many stories begin with a paragraph (or, in some cases, several) of background information about the organisation or the subject of the press release. It's almost as though the writer is thinking: unless the readers understand the basics of the subject, they won't know what I'm talking about. So journalists often see introductions like this: "Ever since telecommunications companies signed licences to offer third generation services – which give the chance for users to access multimedia on their mobiles – individual firms have been looking for ways to differentiate their offerings." And so on and on. Eventually, we get round to the point that the company in question has introduced a service that lets users play Sudoku on their mobiles. So why not write: "Subscribers to Moby's premium service can now play Sudoku between calls." If this is a release for the trade press, you can get down to the detail of why this is important for Moby as a market differentiator in later paragraphs. If it's for the consumer press, you can add facts about why it will be attractive to users.

Trap 3: working up to it. This type of intro is the press officer's equivalent of the magician who is teasing his audience about whether or not he'll be able to pull the rabbit out of his hat. It goes something like this: "There should be big crowds round Speedy Cars stand at the Motor Show next Thursday. For months, the trade press has been filled with rumours about a new model. Managing director Jack Plastered has announced he'll be at the show, but won't say any more. So will there be a new model or won't there?" And so on until nobody particularly cares either way. A press release shouldn't be turned into a guessing game. The story – in this case the launch of the new car – should be in the first paragraph. If it's too early to announce it, then hold fire with the release until it isn't.

Trap 4: potted history. The problem here is that the writer thinks readers can't possibly appreciate the significance of the story unless they know all the salient facts about the organisation behind it. This leads to large amounts of background information being packed into the first sentence, often at the expense of crowding out facts about the real story. So we get intros like this: "Megamoney, the high-street bank formed last year from the merger of Loadsadosh plc and Moneybags International, and which has 3,200 UK branches together with retail and wholesale banking operations in 27 other countries, as well as financial services businesses in insurance, mortgages, saving accounts and credit cards and is an associate of the Far East Banking Conglomerate (except in Singapore)…" At which point you might, if you're lucky, get to the story. When it's necessary to explain what the organisation is in the first sentence – and it's not always necessary – keep the description to an absolute maximum of four or five words.

Trap 5: over-claim. This is the release which looks as though it's got a good story, but which falls away when the journalist digs beneath the surface. It will usually be topped with a sensational headline and the intro will be stuffed with hot words: "Nine out of ten wives want to kill their husbands is the shocking finding of new research." It's only when you dig down onto the second page that you find that although nine out of 10 wives had said in exasperation at some point in their married lives that they'd like to kill their husbands, they had assured the researchers they never meant it really because they actually loved the old boys to bits. Normally, this type of release lacks essential information about the basis of the research. But journalists who call up and insist on an answer learn that the researcher spoke to 17 women at a bus queue in Hartlepool on a wet night in November, by which time they've lost interest in the so-called story.

Avoiding elephant traps such as these will get you at least half of the way to writing that grabby intro which will have a journalist wanting to read on. But you need to do more than avoid getting it wrong. You need to get it absolutely right. So focus again on what is the core of your story. Think about how you can put that into a few simple words. Try different formulations until you are satisfied with what you've written. Don't assume you've done the best you can first time around.

The biggest reason why press officers make a mess of intros is that they try to cram too much information into one sentence. Journalists have a secret weapon for dealing with this problem. It's known by different names but I've always called it the "three par drop". It works something like this. Suppose you're writing a story about an unknown company, started by a brilliant inventor, which is launching a new kitchen gadget – you put in potatoes and get out freshly cooked chips. The problem is you want to describe the gadget, the company and the inventor. Your opening sentence then becomes overloaded like this:

Chipmaster, the company started by William Pointyhead, professor of engineering at the University of Chipping Sodbury, is launching WonderChip, a new kitchen gadget that makes freshly fried chips from unpeeled potatoes.

In a sense, the sentence does the job in that it contains the story. But at 31 words, it is very long and it lacks a sense of momentum to carry the reader on. A "three par drop" approach would read something like this:

A new kitchen gadget which turns unpeeled potatoes into freshly fried chips has just been launched.

WonderChip was invented by William Pointyhead, professor of engineering at the University of Chipping Sodbury.

Professor Pointyhead has set up Chipmaster, a company that will sell the machine direct to chip eaters.

That version runs out at a longer 47 words but it delivers each piece of information in a bite-sized chunk and it also provides a sense of momentum to carry the reader deeper into the story.

The three par drop is not the only way to write intros. But whichever approach you adopt, you should be absolutely certain that it does the job. If it doesn't, you'll have lost your reader by the end of the paragraph.

Step 7: Write the rest of the copy

If you've written your intro well, you'll find it much easier to write the rest of the release. That's because you've already got the main point of the story into the first sentence (or three sentences if you've used the three par drop). You should then use the rest of the information in descending order of importance. How do you decide what is more important?

The guiding principle is to use your information in an order which enables the reader to understand the story most easily. In doing this, keep two over-riding points in mind. First, focus, focus, focus on what your reader wants to know – remember, that your reader is not only the journalist who will receive the release but the people who will read the publication in which your story finally appears.

Thinking about your readers will guide you to how much "context" to give to your release. Most press releases fail to get the question of context right. Some contain no context at all so that it's difficult for a journalist, even with a reasonable knowledge of the subject, to gauge the significance of the story. Others overload the story with so much contextual detail that the story gets lost amidst the background information. It shouldn't be too difficult to judge how much contextual information to add. Think about what your reader is likely to know already and what more he needs to know in order to understand the significance of your story.

But context isn't only about understanding. Using context sensibly can actually strengthen a release. For example, if you can relate what your organisation is doing to something that's happening in the wider world you may be able to make your release piggy-back on a running story that a journalist is already covering. (We'll look at this in more detail on page 107.)

The second over-riding point to keep in mind is never to lose sight of Kipling's "honest serving men" – what, why, when, how, where, who. You should make sure you've answered the questions journalists would want answered in order to decide whether to run a story based on your release. But, on the other hand, don't fall into the trap of descending into the kind of excruciating detail that leads to over-writing and makes your release sound pedantic.

You must balance providing all the required information with the necessity to write briefly.

When you have completed your first draft of the release, there is a simple test you can apply to see whether you've written it logically and as succinctly as possible. Cut the last paragraph and see whether what remains of the story still hangs together. Then cut successive paragraphs from the end and test how far the release holds up. Every time you cut a paragraph from the end, the rest of the release should still read like a complete story – even when you've cut right back to the first three paragraphs. If it doesn't, you've not used your information in descending order of importance and you've not put the main point of your story where it should be – up there in the introduction.

Step 8: add a note to editors (if needed)

Some press releases benefit from having a "note to editors" added at the end. The note gives an opportunity to provide some added detail about the organisation or people mentioned in the release, or about the main subject of the release, that would have over-burdened the main story. It also gives an opportunity to provide more information about the context of the story or about some of the players in the story.

Unfortunately, most "notes to editors" are not used wisely. They tend to consist simply of promotional copy extolling the wonders of the organisation or product which has already been described effusively in the main body of the release. This is a wasted opportunity. A sensible "note to editors", which provides relevant additional information, may actually raise the chance of a release being used or being filed away for future use, perhaps in an upcoming feature dealing with a topic related to your story.

Step 9: Write the headline

At last it's time to write the headline. Perhaps all the while you've been writing the release, your mind has been racing – trying to think of a clever and witty headline. Don't bother. Ninety-nine times out of 100, the best headlines are those that do the job in a simple and straightforward way. Tricksy headlines designed to amuse or tease simply annoy journalists. When they read the headline they're not looking for a laugh – they're looking for a story.

There is another reason why you should choose a straightforward approach. If journalists decide to use the story, they'll want to write their own headlines. Few, if any, will use the headline you've put on the story. If you do happen to headline your story in an apt or amusing way, you've immediately killed that idea for most of the journalists who'll receive your release. They'll know everybody else has got the same release so will steer clear of the headline you've provided.

The headline should be straightforward but it should also attempt to arouse the interest of those jaded journalists who will cast their world-weary eyes over it. A good formula is to use a summary plus fact. For example, the headline

Megamoney Bank posts record profit

does the job in a rather weak way but lacks any significant fact – the "record profit" is unspecified – for the journalist to grab hold of. An alternative is:

Megamoney Bank posts record £328m profit

The addition of the figure lights up the headline and makes

journalists who receive the release realise that you're talking about serious money.

The same approach can be made to work for practically any kind of press release as the following pairs of headlines reveal:

Jones Builders appoints chief executive
Jones Builders appoints former footballer chief executive

Record entries for flower show
Largest ever pumpkin among record flower show entries

In cases where the release contains a complex story or one with a number of equally important points, there is a case for writing a headline with one or two subheads. For example the headline

Most doctors want to leave Britain, says survey

certainly peaks the interest but it is unsatisfying because it doesn't answer the question why. This version does better:

Most doctors want to leave Britain, says survey
* Four out of five can earn more abroad
* Half hate working in the NHS

This version shows why doctors want to work abroad. Moreover, it provides journalists with a couple of extra story hooks for their own piece.

When you write a headline, you should usually attempt to include a verb which provides a sense of action. Headlines without a verb can work – on newspapers, journalists call them "labels"

– but, on the whole, they are less effective in press releases.

Use short words in headlines – for example, "need" instead of "requirement", "job" or "work" instead of "employment". When you've written your headline take a critical look at it to see whether there are any words which could effectively be changed to shorter words without distorting the meaning. Don't be afraid to consult a thesaurus for help.

Finally, never use the headline to oversell the story. It may seem tempting – and for a lot of PR people, it's a temptation they give into – to bolster a weak story with a sensational headline. It never works. As soon as journalists start to read, they'll realise they've been conned and they won't thank you for wasting their time. And if you get a reputation for over-selling stories, you will find it harder to get coverage for a strong story when it does come along.

Step 10: Add date and contact details
All press releases should carry a date, although a good many don't. It is quite enough to put the date at the top of the release, perhaps above the headline although there are no hard and fast rules about this.

Some press releases like to start with a dateline: London, 17 February 2006. This is not wrong. It's simply old fashioned and pretentious. English newspapers gave up using datelines like this about the same time flared trousers went out of fashion. Besides while "Los Angeles, 17 February 2006" has a certain attention-grabbing appeal to it, "Pratt's Bottom, 17 February 2006" just sounds ridiculous.

It is vital that journalists should know where to come if they want more information about the story in your press release. This means that, as the author, you need to add your own contact details at the end of the release. The contact details you must include are your telephone number and e-mail address. If you're working for a public relations company, it's useful to add the firm's full postal address. If you've been working on the release with colleagues, add their contact details as well.

If you are issuing the release on behalf of your own organisation, add your own contact details – telephone number, e-mail address and address of your offices. Add contact details of any other people in your organisation who may be willing to give additional comment. If your organisation has a website, it does no harm to give its address at the end of the release.

Step 11: Add a note about other resources

In the days of electronic communication, it's much easier to provide other resources for journalists such as photographs, charts or background papers. Unfortunately, for some PR people, it can prove a little too easy and some e-mail distributed releases arrive with all manner of unwanted attachments (of which Powerpoint presentations are the most hated). We'll come on to the question of distribution in more detail in chapter 12 page 140, but as a general rule if you're sending your press release by e-mail, it's best not to include any attachments unless they've specifically been asked for in advance or you know for a fact that the publication would welcome them – for example, a magazine that always likes a picture with a story. However, that doesn't mean you can't add a note at the end of your release about the other resources available, including detail about how to obtain them.

Step 12: Edit your release

When you've written your press release and decided you're satisfied that you've presented the story you wanted to tell in the way you wanted to tell it, it's tempting to think that you've finished the job. But even a well-written press release will benefit from judicious editing – and one that's not so well written will definitely need it.

You can certainly edit your own release, if there's nobody else to do it. But it would probably be helpful if you could get a trusted colleague to take a look. Whoever is doing the editing job, there are a number of points to watch out for. First, have you provided all the information that journalists will need in order to use the story? Have you answered all the who, what, why, where, when and how questions or are there any loose ends left hanging in the story?

Have you checked all the facts? It's not enough to assume that facts are correct or to believe they are. You need to know your facts are correct and you need to check them at the primary source – or as close to the primary source of the information as you can reasonably get. It is by no means unknown for senior people to complain about inaccuracies in press coverage of their organisation only to discover the inaccuracy originated from a mistake in one of their own press releases. (In one case, a firm of chartered accountants described itself as a firm of chartered surveyors!)

Next, go through the release and remove all the blatant self-promotion and puffery. Every claim you make in the release should be capable of being substantiated by fact. So if you claim you're the largest supplier of bathroom taps in the world, that's fine as long as you can point to market research evidence which substantiates the claim. If you claim in your release that you're the best supplier of bathroom taps in the world, that's an opinion which you may justifiably hold but with which others may disagree. It shouldn't be in a factual news story, so cut it out.

As you edit, you should be looking for ways to tighten up your release without losing any essential information. As a general rule, even a good writer should be able to cut word length by five per cent after an edit – a poor writer by much, much more.

Step 13: get your press release approved

It is probable that you will be drafting your release in an organisation that has an approval process for press releases. You need to submit your release to this process and deal with any comments. This may cause no problems if you have set up and defined the approval process carefully (as described in chapter four). However, the approval process is a time when all your careful work can unravel if other people in the organisation (or in your client organisation, if you are working for a PR agency) decide they have other ideas.

The worst case is that the approver decides you've completely missed the point of the story. Perhaps you have. And if you have, there is no alternative to going back to the beginning of the research and briefing process and starting again. On the other hand, the approver may think you have missed the point because he or she doesn't understand what a press release is. When this problem occurs, it's not uncommon to discover that what the individuals concerned are actually looking for is something akin to a piece of sales literature. If this is the case, you have to adopt a professional approach and explain plainly what can and can't be achieved with a press release.

More normally, the approval process usually throws up some minor suggested amendments. You should deal with these on a case by case basis. Don't necessarily assume that amendments are unhelpful – they may actually add a snippet of useful extra information or explain a point more clearly. On the other hand, in organisations which have a suspicion of the media, amendments may be designed to remove detail and make the release more bland. Again, you have to deal with these on a case by case basis. The best approach is to try to get to the root cause of the change and see if that can be addressed without making the press release less interesting.

In practice, you will find that you remove many potential problems from the approval process by setting up a professional system for researching, writing and approving press releases at the outset and getting top management support for that process.

Step 14: conduct a final check

Once the release has been approved and any final amendments included, you are nearly ready to issue your release. But not quite. You need to complete one final check to make sure that no errors have crept in during the approval process. And you need to have the release proofread by at least two people with more than a passing knowledge of English and good attention to detail. At last you are ready to issue your press release.

Unless, of course, you want to discover ways to make it even more interesting to journalists. In which case, you had better turn to the next chapter right away.

Chapter 9

Beyond basics: delighting editors

If you follow the 14-step approach outlined in the previous chapter, you should be able to write press releases that meet editors' basic needs. At least, you won't be irritating them with irrelevant and poorly written material.

But we live in a competitive world and, as we've seen in chapter two, some journalists receive hundreds of press releases a week. It's perfectly possible to write and send a competent press release and find that it's ignored. Or, perhaps, not used, which is not quite the same thing. So what extra can you do to make your own release stand out more?

Tailored to fit

The first is to tailor it. Even among broadly competent press releases, most are written to appeal to a range of publications. For example, a release sent out to business, trade and technical publications, might go to some management magazines, computer newspapers, electronics journals and engineering titles. Depending on what the story is, there is no reason why a range of publications such as these shouldn't be interested in different aspects of it. However, if you send just one release, the journalists on each must mine it for their own angle on the story. That angle won't necessarily be right upfront in the first paragraph hitting them between the eyes. So the first action you could take is to write four versions of the release – for each of the management, computing, electronics and engineering publications.

The key point when you are tailoring a release is that you need to think carefully about which element of the story will be of most interest to each group of publications. Bring that out and put it at the front of the release in your introduction. If you write the body of the release carefully enough, you'll find that you can write a number of different introductions which then lead into the body copy. Each of the introductions will present the main point of the story in a way which most appeals to the target publications' point of view. Journalists do sometimes get releases that are tailored at this level, but it's comparatively rare.

The next level of tailoring is even rarer – which is to tailor your release to a single publication or sub-group of publications within a particular market-place. And this is so rarely done that if you can do it well, you could immediately gain a significant competitive advantage over other PR people. If you look at any group of seemingly similar publications with a critical and enquiring eye, you will soon see that they all have a different "editorial voice" – sometimes subtle, sometimes significant. They will have a clear focus on a particular category of readers and how they are seeking to serve them. This is true of national newspapers and consumer magazines as much as business and trade titles. Look, for example, at publications in areas as diverse as women's interest, photography, fishing and homes and you'll see significant differences in editorial approach as each publication seeks to "segment" the market so that it can "own" its own niche.

One of the best ways of discovering how publications segment their markets is, of course, to look closely at several recent copies of the publications in question. But if you don't have time to do that with all the publications in your sights, you can turn to British

Rate and Data – or BRAD, as it's known for short (contact details on page 164) – which is essentially the standard work for the advertising profession. It lists practically every publication in the UK that accepts advertising and provides a simple statement of its target market and editorial focus.

Tailoring your press release for individual publications is often more a case of editing and rearranging your information rather than substantial rewriting. You need to make sure you've presented the main point of your story in a way that is most relevant to the target readers of the publication concerned. Sometimes you can do this as simply as changing the language you use. If, for example, you're sending a release to women's magazines, your intro could variously begin:

A new range of healthcare supplements for young mothers has been launched by…

A new range of healthcare supplements for time-poor thirtysomethings has been launched by…

A new range of healthcare supplements for the older professional woman has been launched by…

Of course, if you're going to adopt this approach, you have to make sure that your story will stand up. This means you need at least one paragraph of supporting information close to the top of the story which supports the specific assertion you've made in your intro. It's important to understand that tailoring is not just a question of changing names as in:

An in-car navigation system for Birmingham motorists has been launched by…

An in-car navigation system for Manchester motorists has been launched by…
An in-car navigation system for Plymouth motorists has been launched by…

Editors will see through that right away. If tailoring is to work, there have to be substantive facts in the body of the copy which support the specific intro of each version of the release. Moreover, those facts need to be rearranged in each version of the story so the most relevant come close to the top of each version of the release.

Adapting press releases at this kind of micro-level can have two very useful effects. First, it can force you to look more closely at the story you've actually got to tell. It makes you refine the story and tell it in a sharper and more focused way. Secondly, it can also make you realise that you really haven't got a story for a particular publication or group of titles after all. That, in itself, can prove a valuable exercise.

HIT THE RIGHT SPOT

Most newspapers and magazines have regular spots in each issue that are given over to a particular topic. You can see a list of some of the most common of these on page 80. Regular spots may range from a full-scale separately bound supplement to a regular page or pages – or even just a column – in the main body of the publication. Knowing about the regular spots in the publications you most want to target can help you to get extra coverage, especially if you write the material with the spot in mind. In a sense, this is another version of tailoring – but it's tailoring with a particular part in the publication in your sights rather than the magazine or newspaper as a whole. As such, you need to have a very clear view of what's needed by that spot before you write something aimed at it.

Take the case of the common example of new appointment announcements. Columns or sometimes pages of these are carried in many publications ranging from local evening and weekly newspapers through to trade and technical publications. Many PR people seem to send the same story to both. The chances are that the way it's written will suit neither. The local paper will be looking for an emphasis on the new appointee's local and community connections. The trade or professional publication will want more about the individual's career, professional qualifications and so on. The fundamental raft of information needed in a release for each is completely different.

But the differences could run even deeper than that. The local newspaper – with plenty of column inches to fill each week – might be looking for half a column, the trade and tech mag with 40 appointments to cover in each issue, no more than one or two paragraphs. So the ideal length for each is different too.

The same principle applies to targeting any regular slot in any publication. You need to develop a deeper understanding of the kind of stories run in that spot, the sort of information needed in the story and the way they're treated in terms of style and approach – for example, are pieces in this slot written in a light or humorous style (such as in a social diary) or are they more formal, even stylised, such as a column of companies' financial results?

But if you're planning to adopt this approach, there is a potential downside you must avoid. Because targeting a specific spot in a publication means giving your release more profile, you have to make sure that you get it exactly right. You must be convinced in your own mind that your story is strong enough and that you've handled it the right way. Paradoxically, journalists can feel even more let down by material that nearly (but not quite) makes it than by a release that misses the point by a mile. They won't have spent any time at all considering the latter, but they may have devoted some of their precious time to trying to make the former stand up. When it falls down – as I know from my own experience – the frustration is palpable.

PIGGY-BACK ON RUNNING STORIES

A "running story" is a story which develops from one issue of a publication to another. In fact, in the age of 24-hour news, it can develop by the hour or even the minute on broadcast media, such as the news channels. A running story could be pretty much anything from a major rail accident and its aftermath, the visit of an overseas leader to the country, to the planning and execution of a major sporting event (such as the 2012 Olympics in London which will, no doubt, provide PR people with abundant opportunities for piggy-back releases).

Piggy-backing on a running story is essentially the black art of linking your own story to the main story, so that it seems to become a bit-part player in the main action. I call this a black art because, although PR people often attempt the trick, it is rarely done well. The most common fault is that the link between the PR story and the running story is simply too tenuous (or, in some cases, non-existent). The effect can become faintly ridiculous, like pinning a red nose on a bishop, or – if the running story is a serious one – faintly sinister, like reciting a black mass over a tomb. So the first step in piggy-backing on a running story is to make sure that there is a genuine and robust relevance in the material you're planning to hoist on to the running story's back.

Once you've established that, you need to use your judgement about whether it is wise to try to piggy-back on the running story. There are a number of reasons why it might not be. For a start, the running story might have elements of tragedy associated with it. Seeking to piggy-back on it could come across as crass bad taste. Then the running story might be moving too fast for you to catch the moment. With a fast-moving story, there's little point in issuing information about something that might have been of interest a week (or even a couple of days) ago. Finally, you might be uncertain about which way events will move. Perhaps they could move in an unexpected direction which could leave your element of the story exposed to criticism. However, if you are thinking about piggy-backing, there are three main areas you might consider.

The first effective way to piggy-back on a running story is to have an "expert" in the subject – if your organisation has such a person – issue a quote commenting on some aspect of the running story, perhaps offering new insight or previously unknown facts. This is a technique which politicians are adept at – they issue comments after (and sometimes before) important government announcements. Often, those comments get picked up by journalists looking for an alternative view on the story. The key point about any quote, however, (as we shall discover on page 114) is that it must serve up some useful new information or provide an insight that is given genuine authority by the person speaking the words. Trite anodyne quotes of meaningless phrases are a waste of everybody's time.

The second common form of piggy-backing is when a product is being used – or, more commonly, has been used – in the running story. Making a success of this is largely a question of timing (see the next sub-section). Frequently after a big event, editors receive a release that reads along these lines:

Shine-o, the biodegradable cleaning fluid, was used to polish the Queen's crown before the State Opening of Parliament.

The problem with this is that the event has passed. Journalists have moved on. You will raise the chances of your story being used if you can time your release to arrive before the deadline of the last edition of the publication before the event.

The third common way of piggy-backing is if a member of your organisation has been involved in some other event or activity as in:

Fred Greenfingers, chairman of the Little Potting Allotment Society, will judge the giant marrows at the County Show next month.

The purpose of this type of piggy-backing is to bring out the expertise of the individual concerned and show that your organisation – in this case, the Little Potting Allotment Society – has people with such skills. You will raise the chances of the story being used if you can add some extra information which the journalist writing the story hadn't got from the primary source. In the example above, for instance: "Mr Greenfingers said that this year he will judge marrows partly on their girth rather than their length."

In a story which several publications may be covering, information from secondary sources appeals to journalists because it provides a potential way for them to get something others don't have.

AT THE RIGHT TIME

Some press releases turn up in the right place but at the wrong time. We have already dealt with the question of making sure that releases arrive in time to meet relevant deadlines. Here, we deal with another aspect of timing which is used by some PR people but generally under-exploited. That is the ability to time a press release to coincide with an event in the calendar.

That event could be something as universal as Christmas or Easter or it could be something very specific – such as a sporting event, an election, the opening of a major film, an annual conference or the anniversary of a national or local organisation. In linking stories to events, you need to follow the same basic principles as for running stories – the link must be genuine and robust although it may not be obvious. In fact, if it isn't obvious it may be more likely to be used.

In the days when I spent some of my time writing press releases for PR firms, I put together a story for a software company that sold a package which, among other things, tracked employees' attendance at work. The release focused on how many employers would end up paying employees more than they needed because they couldn't track absenteeism accurately over the Christmas and New Year period. It was packed with facts and figures about the problems that seasonal absenteeism caused companies. The period between Christmas and New Year is traditionally a slow one for business writers and they're often scratching around for stories. This release provided the foundation for a front-page lead in the Financial Times.

When it comes to timing, you need to ensure that your release is not too early and not too late (but always well ahead of deadline). It may be acceptable to send a Christmas story to a daily paper in the first couple of weeks of December, but it won't be for a weekly or a monthly. Indeed, the monthly could need that story as early as August. One reason why many PR people miss out is that they fail to think ahead and prepare material in enough time. You should consider setting up a calendar of possible events which might provide you with publicity leverage. Then you need to back-track to the deadline dates of the publications to which you'll be sending the material and make sure you get it to them in plenty of time.

In many cases, publications announce their intention to run features in advance. You can simply ring up publications which are relevant to you and ask them for a future features list or you can subscribe to one of the services which compile such lists (see page 160).

OFFER AN EXCLUSIVE

Could you get a better result by offering your news story to one publication rather than issuing it to many as a press release?

Yes, you could, but there are dangers as well as opportunities in this strategy and you need to be aware of both. The opportunity is that a publication – perhaps a magazine or newspaper which is key to reaching your audience – could give the release much more space and prominence than if it turned up like hundreds of others in the editor's inbox. The other side of the coin is that, as a result, it may not receive much, if any, coverage in publications in which you would normally have expected to see some column inches. Perhaps you can live with that.

But you must be careful not to create hostility from other editors. Experienced editors know the score and that they're going to be as much scooped against as scooping. Mostly they will shrug their shoulders, perhaps with a hint of ill-grace, and move on. But if the story is one that their publication couldn't ignore without looking inept they may run a negative or unhelpful version of it. You need to judge the likelihood of that happening before you offer an exclusive. And if you do, you need to be even-handed over the years with your exclusives between the core publications you're seeking to reach. If an editor feels he is being permanently left on the outside, it's not likely to help you foster good long-term relations.

In fact, the biggest problem with the "exclusives" which PR people offer editors is not accepting them but turning them down. The fact is that many PR people simply don't understand the weight a story has to carry before it becomes worth treating as an exclusive. Over the years of working for numerous newspapers and magazines, I've lost count of the number of PR people who've rung with "exclusives" that are so risibly weak it's difficult not to laugh over the phone. So before calling an editor with a hot story, take off your rose-tinted spectacles, look at the story in the cold light of day, and take a down-to-earth decision about whether it really is exclusive material.

PRESS PACKS UNPACKED

If you have a truly important story to tell, you could consider producing a press pack. A press pack, as the name suggests, consists of a collection of material designed to tell the story and provide supporting information. Journalists can find press packs useful when they are planning to write a lot about a particular subject and they need a fair amount of background information to be able to do so authoritatively. But, unfortunately, too many press packs are loaded with sales or promotional literature which often doesn't give journalists the kind of fact-based information they're looking for. If you are planning to put together a press pack, you should consider the following possible items in it:

Lead release. This will give the main story and should be written following the 14-step approach described in chapter eight.

Supporting release. You can consider including a supporting release. There are a number of reasons you might want to do so. If your story involves other organisations apart from your own – for example, where two or more companies are co-operating on a project – the other organisation might want to tell the story from its point of view. If your story is likely to be of interest to different kinds of publications, you might want to produce a range of tailored releases giving the specific detail that will be of interest to each type. Include only the relevant release in each targeted press pack.

User information. Where your release concerns a new product, you may want to include a separate release about the first customers and what they will be using the product for.

People profiles. If there are one or more people who are important in the story – and who will be mentioned in the lead release – you might want to include separate people profiles about them. It is not necessary to include profiles of minor players in the story. Any profile you do include should be more than a souped-up CV. The profile should be focused around the main story and show why the individual concerned is important to the project or activity the main story describes.

Company or organisation backgrounder. You may want to include some information about the company's background. Backgrounders tend to be badly written because they become little more than paeans of praise for everything the organisation has done in the past. What journalists will be looking for are essential facts and figures about the organisation, preferably presented without any unnecessary comment about how wonderful your organisation is.

Graphics. If your press pack is coming in hard copy format, you may want to include photographs of key players, customers, diagrams or charts, as relevant. It's best not to go overboard with this as you can just overload the press pack. Rather, provide information about where editors can obtain images electronically to support any stories they plan to run.

The whole pack should contain comprehensive contact information. If you're sending your press pack through the post – or handing it out at a press conference – there is no reason why it shouldn't be contained in a smart folder. But there is no need to go overboard with these. I've seen press packs in glossy presentation boxes with all manner of fripperies and free gifts, such as pens and notepads, but which on delving deeper seem to provide little or no useful information. I've also been slipped press packs in brown paper envelopes which turn out to contain gold-dust. It's not what it looks like, it's what's in it that matters.

Quote... unquote

When we looked at the 14-stage approach to writing a press release, we touched only briefly on the subject of quotations – or "quotes" as journalists tend to call them. That's because they form a subject which deserves to be dealt with by itself.

Not to put too fine a point on it, most quotes used in press releases are self-serving rubbish. They either state the obvious, or repeat something that's already mentioned earlier in the story, or make a comment which is so bland that it's hardly worth considering. A typical example will crop up in a release about a company which has won a new client. Inevitably, the managing director will be quoted as saying something along these lines: "We are delighted to have Bloggins as new clients." Well, that's a shock!

It is a useful discipline to apply the Roy Jenkins test to quotes used in press releases. The late Jenkins pointed out that the value of any statement made by a politician could be tested by seeing whether the exact opposite would make nonsense. Thus the politician who opines: "I am delighted by the fall in the number of deaths on the roads," is saying nothing useful. Nobody is going to be delighted by an increase in deaths on the roads (with the possible exception of undertakers, and they'll keep their morbid glee well hidden). Thus, because our managing director would not say: "We are not delighted to have Bloggins as new clients," the quote is a waste of space. Much better to write a quote which adds a useful extra piece of information: "Bloggins is the fourteenth new client we've signed up this month."

A related problem with quotes is company functionaries praising their own products or services to the skies. Again, few if any publications are going to publish quotes from the managing director describing his product as the best thing since toasted ciabata. So don't have him say: "Our widget is the most innovative on the market." He could say: "We won last year's Widget Manufacturing Association's award for product innovation."

A high proportion of quotes in press releases exclude themselves from publication on the grounds of either the empty-phrase or the self-praise faults. The trouble is that some of the quotes that do provide useful extra information also don't lend themselves to easy use in the free-flowing pieces journalists tend to write. That's because they read as though they've been generated by a robot rather than a fully paid-up member of the human race. "Forward projections indicate sales commensurate with the preceding annual out-turn," is not the kind of sentence you normally hear dropping naturally from somebody's lips. "We expect to sell about the same as last year," might be.

Let's be clear: journalists like quotes. They make stories human. They provide different points of view. But the quotes must have something useful to say and they must say it in a way that sounds both natural and convincing.

Chapter 10

Putting on the style

If you enrol in one of the many creative writing courses now springing up at universities around the country, it won't be long before your tutor gives you an important piece of advice: show don't tell.

It's a moot point whether press releases come under the heading of "creative writing" – perhaps some are too creative by half – but the advice holds good. Press releases which show the key elements of the story are likely to read more convincingly than those that tell.

What's the difference between showing and telling? "British Airways is the world's favourite airline" is telling. "British Airways carries more passengers than any other airline in the world" is showing. (BA may or may not carry more passengers, but for the purpose of this illustration it does.) Showing involves supporting a statement with evidence so that the reader can see it is demonstrably true. Telling usually involves making an *ex cathedra* pronouncement which may or may not be true (the reader has no way of knowing).

The problem with most press releases is that they spend too much time telling and not enough time showing. It's not difficult to see why. The writers are so wrapped up with their own organisations and have so convinced themselves of the worth of what they're doing, they think they only need to tell other people and they'll have won new converts. When it comes to journalists – world-weary, seen-it-all-before and often cynical – it won't. The journalists to whom you send your release won't have the same enthusiasm for your organisation and its products and services as you do yourself. In fact, they will probably have no enthusiasm for them. They don't want to be told how wonderful your organisation is – they want to be shown and convinced.

How can you get out of the frame of mind which makes you write in a telling rather than a showing mode? It's not easy if the former is ingrained. It will be easier if you keep Kipling's six honest serving men (see page 59) at the front of your mind at all times. The style you should be aiming for is the same that you'd adopt if you were trying to explain how a complicated machine worked or preparing to give evidence in a court case. In the first case, it wouldn't be enough to say how good the machine was at doing its task. You'd need to show which levers to pull or which buttons to press and explain the function of each and the order in which they had to be operated. If you were giving evidence in court, you'd need to describe not what you *thought* but what you *saw*. (So not: "The defendant was blind stinking drunk", but: "The defendant was lying in the gutter drinking from a near-empty bottle of whisky.")

Learning this lesson is important. If you let your press releases show what your story is all about, rather than tell, you should see your column centimetres soar.

FIRST IMPRESSIONS

First impressions are said to be important and this is definitely the case for press releases. As we discovered in chapter two, some releases simply don't even get opened on-screen while others sent by post head straight for the bin without the envelope even being opened. First impressions are created by what your press release looks like. Believe it or not, an experienced journalist will be able to tell at a glance by how your release looks whether it comes from somebody who knows what they're doing.

As releases arrive by two different routes – post and e-mail – we need to consider each separately because the first impressions of both count, but in different ways.

Post

The number of releases that turn up courtesy of the Royal Mail is declining, but can still be a significant number in the offices of some newspapers, magazines and broadcasting organisations. Let's start with the basics. The release should be printed on white A4 paper. Contrary to popular belief among some PR agencies, it's not necessary to have elaborately printed paper for press releases. The release simply needs to be headed with the organisation's name and the words either "Press release" or "News release". Another formula which can be effective is "News from (name of your organisation)".

You should leave the top third of the first page blank except for the heading (as above) and the headline. You start the text about two-thirds of the way down the first page. Make sure the text of the main body of the release is double-spaced and leave a margin of a good two centimetres on either side of the paper. It's acceptable to have a note to editors or further information at the end of the release in single spacing. Number the folios (if there is more than one) and include the word "more…" followed by three "leaders" (full stops) at the bottom of each page except the last. Include the word "continued…" with three leaders at the top of each new page except the first. End the release with the word "end". Don't indent the first paragraph, but indent all following paragraphs with two or three spaces. Don't leave a line between paragraphs. Staple rather than paperclip the pages together. All this is basic stuff, but it's surprising how many releases get one, some or even all of them wrong.

E-mail

With releases delivered by e-mail, it's been possible to abandon some of the rules applied to paper releases. However, a number of features which journalists don't find helpful have grown up in the world of cyberspace. Let's look first at the paper-based conventions which can or cannot be abandoned. It's rare to see an e-mailed press release double-spaced. Journalists have mixed views about this. Some think that as the release is going to be handled electronically, it doesn't matter. Others think that it's easier to read on-screen if it is double spaced. It's hardly necessary in an e-mailed release to use the footers and headers "more..." and "continued". So, in theory, it should be easier all round for PR people to send and journalists to receive e-mailed releases. Except that a whole range of practices have grown up which don't help the journalists. The first is the practice of including elaborate headings at the top of the release. Inevitably, these take a few irritating extra microseconds to download and can cause problems when a journalist is seeking to manipulate the core text electronically.

But the most common complaint about e-mailed releases is about the excessive use of complex formatting. Just because it's possible to use large text, different fonts, bold text, italic text and all manner of other variations doesn't mean you have to. Almost certainly, journalists won't want to include your formatting options if they use the piece, so you're just giving them extra work to remove it. Most journalists are getting wise to the fact that a lot of fancy formatting designed to catch the eye is the PR's equivalent of fur coat and no knickers. In other words, the story is weak. You can format in 72 point bold red type, but it will still be a weak story and journalists will still spot the fact. Best to work on strengthening the story rather than the formatting.

STYLE ESSENTIALS

There are three reasons why style is important in a press release. The first is clarity. Something that is written clearly is easier to understand. Adopting a good style should make what you have to say easier to understand – especially important when you are describing something that is new or unfamiliar to your readers.

The second in familiarity. Although every newspaper and magazine has its own nuances of style, journalists have a broad understanding of the conventions of what kind of writing is acceptable as something of publishable quality. If your release matches up to those conventions, the journalists who receive it will feel more comfortable with it. The style you've used has encouraged them to look deeper at what you've got to say, rather than placing a barrier between you and your audience.

The third is tone. You need to adopt a tone that is appropriate to your subject matter. Most press releases fail to adopt the kind of objective and dispassionate tone about the subject matter which journalists would generally apply to a straight news story. (An opinion piece or feature would be different.) Too often the tone of releases is that of the cheer-leader rather than the neutral spectator. The result is that the release sounds more like a piece of propaganda than a news story.

So what can you do to ensure that you meet the necessary standards on clarity, familiarity and tone? There are a number of important style points which address one or more of the three.

For a start, write simply. Use short words in short sentences organised into short paragraphs. One of the oldest journalist adages is "never use a long word when a short word will do". It should apply equally to press release writers. But a word of warning: be sure the short word does mean exactly what you want it to – sometimes you need the longer word for the sake of precision. Always seek to avoid jargon – look for a common English word rather than the jargon. If using a jargon word is unavoidable because there is no common English equivalent, make sure the jargon word is clearly and concisely explained.

Short sentences work best. But if you do use a long sentence, bear in mind Mark Twain's advice to writers on how to treat them: "At times he [the writer] may indulge himself with a long one, but he will make sure there are no folds in it, no vaguenesses, no parenthetical interruptions of its view as a whole; when he has done with it, it won't be a sea-serpent with half of its arches under water; it will be a torch-light procession."

When you've written your release look for opportunities to break long sentences down into two (or more). But do try to vary the sentence length within reasonable bounds so that the release doesn't sound as though it's being read by a telegram boy on speed.

Next, keep paragraphs short. But try to avoid single sentence paragraphs, except in special cases – for example, where a point is exceptionally important or where the sentence is introducing a list. As H W Fowler, the wise and witty compiler of Fowler's Modern English Usage, puts it: "The purpose of the paragraph is to give the reader a rest. The writer is saying to him: 'Have you got that? If so, I'll go on to the next point.'"

On the general question of style, you can't do much better than take George Orwell's advice (in *Politics and the English Language*, 1946): "A scrupulous writer, in every sentence that he writes, will ask himself at least four questions, thus: What am I trying to say? What words will express it? What image or idiom will make it clearer? Is this image fresh enough to have an effect? And he will probably ask himself two more: Could I put it more shortly? Have I said anything that is avoidably ugly?"

The whole point of giving attention to these broad style points is to make your work more acceptable to the journalists who receive it – and who are, themselves, no neophytes when it comes to handling the English language. By creating an acceptable style, you make your press release more accessible. You increase the chances of it being read. Look on good style as the welcome mat which you lay out for visitors – those editors who are going to read your release. But don't imagine that dealing with style in general terms is enough. You also need to pay attention to detail.

ATTENDING TO DETAIL

Adopting a good style may make your press releases more acceptable to journalists, but style also has some important practical implications which you need to think about.

The first of these is to ensure that journalists refer to essential elements of your organisation in the way you would prefer to have them described. For example, you want to make sure that key personnel in your organisation are referred to by their correct job titles, that products get their correct names, that services you provide are described accurately and that other key company information is referred to consistently. Some companies already have a company style book or, less ambitiously, a style sheet which they use not only for press releases, but for other marketing collateral and business activities generally.

Some press releases hit just the right note in terms of style. They refer to their own activities in a precise, consistent yet succinct and reasonably objective way. But many others make one of two important errors. A minority of releases are written by people who are so laid back they're practically horizontal. They are too lax about referring to pretty much everything in the release. For example, they might quote an individual who is described as the "managing director" at one point, "owner" at another, "founder" at a third and "chairman" at a fourth. It's true the individual might be all four – but what's the journalist on deadline going to call this individual for short? So be aware that if you are not precise about how you describe key points in your release, you're opening the door for journalists to choose their own description.

Far more releases go to the other extreme. They are models of control freakery. Inevitably, the product's name will be spelt out always in CAPITAL LETTERS. Sometimes the name will adopt some weird and wonderful typography – a mixture of upper and lower case letters. Others sprinkle the trademark ™ or copyright © symbols liberally across the text of the release. Then there will be a generous use of capital letters – certainly for job titles (Chief Rat Catcher), probably for events (Annual General Meeting), possibly for corporate facilities (Factory, Offices, Car Park). Key sentences may be picked out in bold text, italics, underlining or, in the worst cases, all three.

However, by far the most common fault of the control freak variety of press release (and some others as well) is the writer's insistence on referring to the organisation by some adulatory, self-serving and frequently tendentious description. Typically a press release starts like this:

Limb Support Ltd, whose Straight Up surgical stockings with miracle fabric GripOElasTic (Firm yet Gentle) are chosen by more over-80s than any other brand in Andorra, Leichtenstein and Sark, has announced…

By the time journalists have waded through the sales message in the opening words of the release, many will have lost interest in what the announcement is. It's much more effective to give the story first and save the background information for later as in:

A surgical stocking, which massages wearers' legs as they go for a walk, has been launched by Limb Support.

You'll note that if you've written the first sentence intelligently, you don't need to waste words on describing the company, because it's obvious from what you've said, what it does. You can add extra company detail further down the story.

The remedy for both the laid back and the control freak is to revert to the happy middle path. Use capital letters sparingly. Most newspapers and magazines do not refer to job titles (with the possible exception of the Queen and the Pope) using capitals. You gain favour from journalists – and save them the task of taking down four letters from upper to lower case – by not doing so when you mention the deputy assistant regional accountant. Do not use bold text, underlining or italics, except in special cases. For example, you could put the name of a book, film or play in italics.

There is no need in a press release to be a slave to style, but you may want to be consistent over the way you present content you regularly use such as numbers, dates, measurements and so on.

In order to find ways to do this, you can consult one of the style guides briefly described in the panel below.

A guide to style guides

Three style guides which can help press release writers are:
New Hart's Rules: The Handbook of Style for Writers and Editors, (R M Ritter, adapter), 2005. This, and its earlier editions, have been the holy writ for printers for generations. It contains everything you're likely to need to know about spelling, punctuation, capitalisation, abbreviations and much more.

Style Guide, The Economist, (2005). This is a wonderful little book which helps you understand why *The Economist* magazine is so well written. The introductory section on "the essence of style" is worth the purchase price alone. There are two other useful sections – American and British English, a fact checker and glossary.

Financial Times Style Guide, Colin Inman, (2000). This invaluable book now seems to be out of print, although it is still possible to buy second-hand copies. It's more of a mini-encyclopaedia of the business world with comprehensive listings of areas such as computing and energy terms, financial markets, jargon, and currencies.

As we discovered in chapter two, many journalists regard the standard of English used in press releases as poor. It is clearly beyond the scope of this book to teach basic English, but if you secretly feel that your written English is a little shaky, you might consider consulting one of the books mentioned in the bibliography on page 158.

However, there are two common errors that crop up so frequently in press releases that we can't move on without dealing with them. These are:

The aberrant apostrophe
Managing director's have been invited to a conference...
Managing directors lifestyle will be the subject of a conference...

Both are wrong, instances of the disease of the "aberrant apostrophe", first identified by author and newspaper columnist Keith Waterhouse. In recent years, the disease has become a pandemic. In the first case, "managing directors" is a plural and does not need a possessive apostrophe. In the second, the lifestyle mentioned belongs to the managing directors, which requires a possessive apostrophe after the "s" as they are plural.

Singular-plural mix-up
The company's board is studying the implications of the share price and they are expected to issue a statement next week.

Is the company's board going to be singular or plural? It can reasonably be either, although singular would be most common in the press and plural in broadcast journalism. In the sentence above, it starts off as singular (note the verb "is") but then becomes plural in the second half of the sentence ("they are"). That's just sloppy English which smacks of amateurism.

Finally, it's heartening to note that most PR people and publicists seem to take care over proofreading their releases before they're issued. But there are still plenty of releases with irritating typos and minor errors which should have been picked up by careful proofing. If you want to improve your proofreading skills, consult the book *Proofreading Plain and Simple*, details in the further reading list on page 159.

Avoiding legal trouble

In focusing on these issues of style, it's important not to lose sight of the question of accuracy. Journalists can and do come across the most glaring factual errors in press releases. Everyone has their own stories to tell. I've seen a release from a well-known public company which wrongly stated that it was listed on a particular stock exchange. When this was duly published, the company's PR director rang the publication to complain about the error. Little more was heard of the complaint after the editor drew his attention to his own press release which contained the inaccurate information.

Of course, to err is human. But I can't stress too strongly the importance of checking all facts. Editors will not thank you for publishing errors. And I know of other journalists who have got into serious trouble by importing press release errors into their own stories. You will certainly damage your reputation for reliability and may find it more difficult to get stories published in the future. So when checking facts ask yourself this question: if I'm asked to justify this, what reference can I give? If you don't have a primary reference or a rock-solid secondary source, think twice about using the information. The old journalist adage applies to press releases: if in doubt, leave out.

However, the question of accuracy is not the only issue of which you need to be aware. Before we move on, we must consider two possible trouble spots you need to avoid in press releases – libel and copyright.

Libel

In most cases, libel is not going to be a major problem for press release writers. Usually, they are writing about their own organisations, products and services – and if defamation slips in they're hardly likely to sue themselves. However, there are some possible dangers, especially if you are planning to refer to competitor organisations or products, perhaps to compare them with your own in an unfavourable light. You need to remember that a corporate body as well as an individual can be libelled. The tests of libel are whether what you've written lowers the standing of the complainant in the eyes of "right thinking" people, whether it exposes them to "hatred, ridicule or contempt", whether it causes them to be shunned or avoided, or whether it discredits their profession, business or trade. So if you are planning to trash a competitor, you need to be absolutely certain of your facts and to present those facts fairly and in context.

If you are sued, you need to prove what you said is true by reference to primary sources – so don't pick up what somebody else has written or rely on rumours. Present what you have to say in careful language – don't throw indefensible adjectives about – and be careful about drawing conclusions from the facts at your disposal. For example, you may know that a rival has just lost its largest customer, but that doesn't necessarily mean you can say that it is in financial difficulties.

There are more potent libel dangers for those writing press releases for campaigning organisations. They may wish to be more forthright in criticism of individuals and bodies which are in their sights. There is nothing wrong with criticism and the law recognises the right of free speech, but statements must be based on fact and proportionate in their use of language.

If you do find that you have run into a libel difficulty, your first step must be to consult a lawyer who specialises in libel even before you've replied to your complainant. In broad outline, there are three defences to libel. The first is that what you wrote is true, but proving the truth of a statement in court is not always as easy as it seems. The second is that what you wrote is "fair comment" on a matter of public interest. But a fair comment must be based on fact, made in good faith and written without malice. The third is privilege, which covers reports of parliament and courts and is not likely to be relevant for press release writers except in rare cases.

Copyright

The law of copyright also provides a few potholes into which the unwary press release writer may stumble. The main problem here is using a quote from another writer's material without acknowledgement. In general, you breach copyright if you quote a "substantial part" of a copyright work without the author's permission. What constitutes substantial depends, in part, on the length of the original work. But it also depends on the quality of the part you have quoted. For example, if you quoted verbatim all of the conclusions of a research report, that might be deemed breach of copyright, because the conclusions are the most important part of the report.

So if you are quoting from other people's work, make sure that you do so reasonably and that you provide an adequate acknowledgement of their work in your release – what is known as "fair dealing". If uncertain, ask the copyright holder for permission to quote.

Chapter 11

Picture power

A picture, according to the old Chinese proverb, is worth a thousand words. And when journalists look at some of the pictures they get sent, many of those words are unprintable.

In fact, journalists' complaints about contributed press pictures tend to fall into two main categories. There are those who get sent pictures – sometimes in massive electronic files – which they don't want because either they don't publish pictures or it's not the kind of picture they would want to publish anyway. And there are those who are annoyed that a story which they'd like to use isn't accompanied by a picture or that the picture which has been sent isn't of high enough technical quality to use.

So how can you source and supply the perfect picture to accompany the perfect release?

Three steps to good pictures

I asked Caroline Duffy, the brilliant freelance magazine designer, what she looks for from contributed photography. She suggests that there are three main aspects to bear in mind when you're supplying photos to a newspaper or magazine. They are the composition of the image, the "technical stuff" and the way the image is supplied. We look at each of these in more detail below. But, first, Caroline advises: "It's vital you use a professional photographer to make sure all three aspects are as good as they can be. An amateurish shot is not going to make your people or products look good and will probably even have a negative effect. Furthermore, the more attractive and creative a shot is, the more likely us creative types will want to use it, and use it as big as possible on the page, thereby getting you even more publicity."

Composition of the image

For shots of people, it's good to have a selection of head, top-half and full-length shots, advises Caroline. The more options designers have, the more likely they are to use the pic and use it big. The background should be neutral and plain – black or white appear the most professional.

Caroline admits that many shots she receives from PR people turn her off. "For some reason PR shots are often of people standing next to the logo of their business – for example, outside the front door of the building and, for me, this is a bit cheesy. I think press releases need to inspire curiosity – the subconscious question 'what's this about?' – and some bloke in a dodgy tie looking uncomfortable next to a front door doesn't rock my boat!"

Obviously, it's important to think about what the subject of the picture is wearing and the image they want to put across. But Caroline argues: "These days it's not always necessary to wear a suit – it depends on what they're selling I guess."

For shots of products, Caroline recommends a white background unless the product is white or a pale colour in which case you should use black. She suggests: "Varied, interesting angles as well as the obvious shot from the front all help the designer to make his/her page look more interesting and they'll use the shot bigger. Avoid coloured lighting – the product must look like the product – just make it look as sexy and interesting as possible. Ask the photographer for advice – explain what you want, the feelings and message you are trying to convey. Perhaps even show the photographer some photos in the style that you'd like to emulate.

"I would recommend that you check out what your competitors are doing with similar products. Try to find out what they're doing well and what they could improve on – look at the benchmark and aim to beat it. And (obviously) if the product has any unique selling points, make sure the photographer gets some nice close-ups of them."

The technical stuff

Before you commission any photography, it is vitally important that you make sure you will have the rights to use the images as you wish. Photographers have different contracts or rules about this, so you must be clear and you should have the question of the rights to use the photos agreed in writing.

After the photoshoot, ask the photographer to colour balance, sharpen and generally touch up any imperfections in the image – whether it's finger marks on a mobile phone or spots on the chin – but don't go too mad with Photoshop (the software package designers and photographers often use for manipulating and editing photography) or it will become obvious that you've "doctored" the shot. But there is nothing wrong with reasonable picture editing – newspapers and magazines do it all the time. As Caroline says: "It's not vanity – it's creating the right impression!"

Newspapers and magazines will all have their own preferences for picture supply and it pays to find out what a particular publication prefers. As a general rule of thumb, photos should be supplied at 300dpi (dots per inch) in CMYK colourspace, as a high-quality compression jpeg or a tiff file. (CMYK stands for cyan-magenta-yellow-black, a method which creates all colours from these four basic coloured printing inks. Jpeg stands for Joint Photographic Experts Group and, in this context, the standard used for the creation of electronic photographic files. Tiff stands for tagged image file format, the most widely supported file format for storing bit-mapped images on PCs.)

Caroline advises: "Photos should be big enough to use at full page size – personally I would recommend the photos be roughly A4 in size. If your photo will need to go on a poster, make sure the photographer's digital camera will take shots that will be big enough – shouldn't be a problem these days – but if the pic needs to go really big you might want to consider having it shot using a medium or large-format-film camera – again, ask the photographer for advice."

She adds: "With product shots we often like to use cut-outs – the product has had the background cut away and we can wrap text around it. Ask your photographer or design agency to put a clipping path around the product so that publication designers can quickly make a cut-out if they need it. A professional looking drop-shadow makes a lot of difference – this is partly good photography but can be done by someone competent in Photoshop – again, the easier you make the designer's life the more likely your pic will be featured prominently. This is not me being lazy, honest! Magazine and newspaper designers have very little time to make their pages look good, and good photography makes them very happy."

The way the image is supplied

The more options you give the designer, the better. But a downside to 300dpi images at A4 size is that the file size will be pretty big – and no-one likes their in-box crammed, no matter what speed broadband they have. So best to have small RGB jpeg files of all your images – no more than 200k each – which you can send out with the press release or to the designer. Make it clear that higher quality versions are available. The best way of supplying these is either e-mailing the ones requested, giving out a link to a website where the images can be downloaded or sending out a CD with all the images on it.

Most designers use Apple Macs, which will read PC format CDs, but PCs will not generally read Apple Mac CDs so if you're using a Mac make sure you burn the CD as a hybrid – so it can be used on both formats – just in case. "And," concludes Caroline, "do not under any circumstances supply images embedded in Word or Powerpoint – the designer will come after you with an icepick."

BRIEFING THE PHOTOGRAPHER

Listening to Caroline's advice, it all sounds pretty straightforward. Why, then, does it seem to go wrong so often? The problem usually starts right at the very beginning with the photographer's briefing (see model picture briefing on page 139).

Julian Hawkins is a top magazine photographer who has seen his work in some of the country's most prestigious publications. He says: "Those who commission tend to have little knowledge of file formats, how a picture will be used, and so on, and therefore don't necessarily give an accurate commissioning brief. They also undervalue what photographers are able to do, regard pictures as being snaps and pay accordingly. If potential usages were thought through, then consideration might be given to the fact that to have pictures of suitable quality to run at half, full or even double page spread size needs more than just a jpeg."

Nick Sinclair, another outstanding photographer whose stunning portraits have graced many magazines, also complains that PR photo briefs are too often not thought through. "Some PR people tend to assume you can read their minds," he says. "It's quite common when you ask them what they want to be told 'do what you normally do'. What's happening in those situations is that they have an image in their mind of what they want and assume it's in your mind as well. They take it for granted that you'll come up with what they want."

When you hire a photographer, it's very important to get a clear idea of what the costs are going to be. Most good photographers will charge for their time by the day (often in increments of half a day for location shooting or, possibly, by the hour for studio shots). On top of that, they'll charge for travel, materials used and processing costs and, sometimes, the use of an assistant, if they're taking a lot of equipment to a location shot. All those extras can add a tidy sum to the basic fee. But it's very important to get an estimate of them when you agree the total cost of the job. Failure to do so only leads to arguments later on and may make it difficult for you to use the photos if the photographer refuses to assign copyright until his invoice is paid. Remember, also, that if you ask the photographer to take one or two extra shots while he's at the shoot, on top of those originally commissioned, he may charge extra for them.

Many of the problems over photography arise because press officers find themselves caught in the middle between what editors want and what their organisation wants to provide. In a lot of companies, senior managers are frightened of the kind of creative photography with attitude – of both themselves and their products – which magazines and newspapers love to publish. As a result, they fall back on the kind of "cheesy" shots which roll into newspaper and magazine offices by the hundred every week. Certainly, cheesy shots do get used, usually because there is nothing better. But if you fall back on cheesy photography you're missing out on an important way in which you can differentiate what you offer the media over what others provide. Quality creative photography is often the factor which draws editors' attention to the story – and which raises the chances that it is used.

MAKING CAPTIONS WORK

A common problem with many photographs received in newspaper and magazine offices is that they lack a caption or, at least, an effective caption which sells the picture and the story which accompanies it. In the old days of prints sent out in board envelopes, captions often used to be pasted on to the back of the print. With pictures in electronic format, you need to include a caption in the accompanying e-mail.

In some cases, it is quite enough if you just provide a caption which covers the basics of who or what the picture is. This is particularly the case when you're sending a picture at an editor's special request. However, do make sure the caption contains all the needed information. You may have provided details in the press release, but if that's already being processed elsewhere, it needs an irritating check to get the details.

If you've sent a picture of a person, you need to include his or her name, together with any job title or position in the organisation. If the picture shows somebody doing something, it ought to state briefly but precisely what he or she is doing – for example, opening the new offices or running in the London Marathon. If there are several people in the photograph, you must make sure the caption names each of them clearly, normally by naming them from left to right as you look at the picture.

When you send a picture of a product, make sure your caption clearly names the product and briefly states what it does. If the picture shows the product doing something, the caption should say what it's doing. Just because you know what it's doing, don't assume a journalist will also know. Any caption should contain the contact details you'd include on a press release.

Although a simple factual caption should suffice for most pictures, there are cases when you may want to write a sharper caption or even an extended caption, especially when the picture is the story. You can make the caption draw attention to the story by summarising the main point in it. For example, if you're sending a picture of a new chairman, instead of just sending the name and job title, you might write a caption like this: "New chairman: John Smith takes up his appointment at Gubbins Corporation on 1 August."

An extended caption comes in useful when you've got an unusual or attractive picture which might make it into print but not a particularly strong story to go with it. There is no point in sending a photo with an extended caption unless you know the publication in question uses them. But if it does, your caption should start as a normal caption, then fill in details of the rest of the story, normally in no more than three or four sentences. This is the kind of thing:

> The smile says it all. Joan Smith holds the cup aloft after winning the ladies' croquet singles at Little Witchering Croquet Club on Wednesday 21 July. Joan, 83, won the cup at her first attempt. She took up croquet after a hip replacement operation last year.

Model picture briefing

Briefing from:

Contact address:

Contact phone:

Contact e-mail:

Photographer's name:

Photographer's contact details:

Location of shoot:

Date of shoot:

Time:

Contact at shoot:

Pictures required:

For use in:

Formats required:

Picture subject:

Must shots:

Other desirable shots:

Style of shots:

Other special instructions:

Agreed fee:

Agreed expenses:

Picture delivery instructions:

Deadline for delivery:

What's clear from talking to editors on all kinds of publications is that PR people are missing out on lots of opportunities to get coverage either by not providing pictures or providing shots which are not good enough. You could well find that giving extra attention to photos will be more than repaid in additional coverage.

Chapter 12

Getting the story out there

So you've written your press release, you've got it signed off and you're ready to send it out to all those newshounds who are just itching to publish it. Or not. What can you do to make sure you distribute it effectively?

The question of distribution is important because it is at this point that some perfectly respectable stories get lost among the heap of drivel which hits journalists' desks. That's not surprising when, as we discovered in chapter two, some publications are receiving more than 500 press releases a week.

Let's start with the fundamentals.

Distribution basics

The most basic point of all is not to send releases to journalists who can have no conceivable interest in them. This is one of the problems which journalists complain about most and it's why journalists approach all press releases with more suspicion than might otherwise be the case. It can't be said often enough: understand the publications and writers you're targeting and send them only material you can be reasonably sure will be of some interest to them. Having said that, let's consider the two main methods of distributing releases – the post and e-mail.

The postman only knocks once

Which, for many editors, is once too often where press releases are concerned. Only a minority of releases are still distributed by post and it's probable that the proportion that arrive courtesy of Her Majesty's mails will continue to decline.

Check the name and address of the journalists to whom you're sending the release and make sure envelopes are correctly addressed (many aren't). On the whole, try to avoid sending releases to "The editor". If you don't even know the name of the journalists you're contacting, it's unlikely you'll know whether they might be interested in your story. Finally, if you're sending a release by post, take into account the amount of time it will need to be delivered, especially if you're trying to hit a deadline.

You've got mail (unfortunately)

Most press releases now arrive by e-mail (and don't they!). On the whole, editors are happy to accept releases by e-mail when the release is about a relevant topic. The trouble is that, because e-mail is a "cost free" distribution channel, it encourages some PR people to blitz everybody in sight, irrespective of whether they are likely to have any interest in the release or not. So e-mail releases are beginning to get – I might say, have got – a bad reputation among some journalists.

It's not surprising that some editors admit that they use their delete buttons freely without even bothering to look at the contents of the releases. Others use spam filters to try to keep the worst of the irrelevant stuff at bay. And, be warned, some of these anti-press release spam filters can be very effective. On a couple of occasions with one well-known magazine, I've even had commissioned features blocked by them!

However, if you use e-mail intelligently, you can build a constructive and helpful relationship with those journalists you particularly want to reach. The starting point is what you put in the "subject box" of the e-mail. Many releases simply repeat the headline. Something along the lines of "Obscure Corporation posts 1% profits rise" is not uncommon. This immediately signals to all who are not interested in the doings of Obscure Corporation that it's of no interest. A sweaty finger reaches for the delete button.

What journalists want is a simple way of recognising stories that may be of interest. What's more, when e-mailed releases come into a busy newsroom, whoever's drawn the short straw of trawling through them wants a quick way to spot which journalist to route them to. So why not signal that in the "subject box"? Jenni Davies, editorial co-ordinator on Maxim, which receives around 1,000 releases a week, advises: "Make your release stand out. Spell out what the release is about – INVITE, CELEBRITY NEWS, MUSIC FOR REVIEW, FASHION LAUNCH, QUIRKY PRODUCT!, BEAUTY BARGAINS. This way it can be directed quickly to the right person."

Next, the format. By far the most favoured approach by journalists is to have the release in the body of the e-mail. In this way, it's simple to read and, if it's used, it can be cut and pasted into whatever story the journalist is writing. There is no need to add fancy graphics – and certainly not photographs or diagrams – to the e-mail which only slow down access time.

On the whole, most journalists don't favour attachments, partly because they take extra time to open. If the story is something a journalist really wants, a Word attachment might just be acceptable because it's a format from which it's easy to cut and paste. But do not send your press release as a PDF file. Unfortunately, more press officers are using this format, presumably because they believe the ability to engage in extra fancy formatting will make their release stand out more. It won't. It's the quality of the story that makes a release stand out. And even though it's now possible to cut and paste from PDF files, the process is not as convenient for editors as having the press release right there in the e-mail.

Should you send a picture as an attachment? That's not an easy decision for you to take as journalists are divided between those who want a picture with the release and those who don't. Some of those publications that use a lot of contributed pictures like to see a low-resolution file of what's available, so they can order the high-res version if they like what they see. Other publications don't want pictures because they use few contributed shots or because the shots they're sent simply don't match the style they use. There is no short-cut here: you simply have to take the time to find out who wants pictures (and what kind) and who doesn't and then organise your distribution accordingly. That might seem like a lot of effort, but then distributing press release material to journalists effectively is.

You may decide to distribute your own press releases. If you're only likely to issue releases occasionally and to a limited number of journalists, this is probably the most effective – and certainly the cheapest – option.

However, if you find that the volume of your release activity imposes a strain on your resources, there are professional distribution services to help you, whether you're distributing your releases by post or e-mail. Details of some of these services are contained on page 163.

HANDLING THE FALLOUT

When you've distributed your release, a number of things may happen. The most common is nothing. Your release will be in a bin or the victim of a journalist's active e-mail delete button. Your story wasn't strong enough or you failed to target.

However, it's conceivable that you will get some feedback. If journalists want to follow up on your release, it's possible you could get that feedback within minutes of the story hitting their desks. That could come most probably in the form of a phone call or, possibly, if you distributed the release electronically, by e-mail. In any event, if your story has hit the spot, it's likely you may get some feedback during the course of the day (in the case of dailies and some weeklies) and within the next few days (in the case of other weeklies and most monthlies).

The first important rule of handling feedback is: be there. It is astonishing how many PR people and publicists send out quite interesting stories and are not available to handle further queries on the day the story hits journalists' desks or PC screens. So if you're handling a story which is likely to generate calls, make sure you've arranged your diary so that you'll be able to take them – at least on the day you issue the release.

The second important rule is to make sure that you've assembled the necessary background information to answer simple factual enquiries which the release might stimulate. Again, it is surprising how many PR people (especially in agencies) can't answer even simple questions about their clients – including no-brainers such as a company's turnover or the name of the chief executive. If you're handling press relations for an organisation, you ought to have a file containing basic facts about it readily to hand.

But if you've just issued a press release which you're hoping will get coverage, you need to do more than that to handle journalists' enquiries effectively. The key point before you've even issued the release is to try and anticipate the kind of questions journalists might ask. You may say that if you've identified information a journalist may want to know it should be in the release. Perhaps it should. But you can't include every fact, in the interests of brevity. And, in any event, some journalists may be interested in one aspect of the story, others in a different aspect. You need to be on hand with the extra details to satisfy both. Indeed, by giving those journalists who call extra interesting bits of information which others haven't asked for, you're likely to improve the showing your story will get if it is used.

The other issue you need to anticipate is whether journalists will want to interview any of the key players mentioned in your press release. Again, this is another potential frustration for journalists, as I know from personal experience. You want to get extra insight and quotes from the managing director/chairman/recipient of the award or whoever, and they're not available. Worse still, the publicist doesn't know when they will be available. So the rule is simple: if further comment is likely to be needed, make sure the key player is available at least on the day the release is issued.

Finally, be certain that your release covers topics on which your organisation is prepared to provide further information. In researching this book, one journalist told me about what happened when he followed up a release from a well-known non-profit making association. The release had mentioned an article in the current issue of the association's newsletter. The journalist thought this could make a piece in his magazine. But when he called he was bluntly told the newsletter was for members only – and he couldn't see it, despite the mention of the story in the release. As he said: "This is seriously stupid behaviour." But that type of incident is by no means unique. If you don't want journalists to know about it, don't mention it in a press release.

Your release overcomes all the hurdles and makes it into print – or at least the main burden of the story is published. Your joy is unconfined. Or perhaps not, if there is an error in the story or you feel it has been presented in a garbled or unhelpful way. Is there anything you can do?

If there is a serious factual error, certainly. You should e-mail or write to the editor of the publication and point out what the error is, why it is damaging, and what the accurate information is. You should ask for a correction in the next available issue of the publication. You should, it goes without saying, do this in a polite and business-like manner. A responsible publication that has made an important error of fact will invariably correct it.

Other cases are more problematical. A journalist may rewrite a story from a press release in a way that gives a take on the story which is not what you were hoping to convey. There is no one hundred per cent guarantee that this won't happen but the way to make it much less likely is to write your story objectively and briefly, eschewing the self-congratulation and puffery that disfigures most press releases. If the story is well written in a style which is acceptable to the journalist, it is less likely he or she will rewrite it or, at any rate, the rewrite may be less fundamental.

On other occasions, you may find that quotes or selected bits of information are taken from your release and used in a story which, perhaps, also mentions other organisations. There is nothing you can do about this. If you have issued a press release, you have effectively placed the information in the public domain. Whether the information has been used fairly or "out of context" is going to be largely a matter of judgement.

However, there is something you can do to guard against your information being used out of context in an unhelpful way.

You need to make sure you've drafted the release is a way that ensures every sentence is unambiguous. Don't write in such a way that invites speculation about what your organisation might or might not do. Ensure that quotes from people in the organisation are self-contained and not drafted in a way that is open to misinterpretation. The fewer hostages to fortune you offer up in the release, the less likely you should find that the information is used in an unhelpful way.

BUILDING A PRESS RELEASE ARCHIVE

Here's a thought: instead of pushing unwanted press releases at journalists, why not pull them towards what you've got to offer? To do this, your organisation needs to become known as a source of useful and reliable information on the subjects about which its people are expert.

In the last few years, it has been noticeable how many organisations have built archives of press releases and other briefing material on their websites – often in special press or media areas. Increasingly, journalists are more inclined to go looking for background material for articles – especially features – on the web. Those companies that get a reputation for building a good archive of useful material can, and do, score.

Essentially, a good archive is one which is easy to find on the website – not all are easy to locate – and where the press material is organised in a sensible and accessible way. On the whole, journalists find it less easy to use archives where releases are stored in PDF files, than those which store the information in simple downloadable HTML files or even as Word docs. Of course, the file is as good as the quality of the releases in it. If the original releases were full of self-promotion and puffery, few journalists are going to spend much time looking for material.

In an archive of press releases, it's very important to make sure that the title of each release clearly summarises the content. There is no room for "clever" or punning headlines. Just stick to the facts. As a whole, journalists researching background will be looking for information around a particular subject, so make sure the main theme of the release shows in the headline in the archive index. Often, journalists are looking for case studies, so it's wise to flag these up as well. And if there are any background papers, it may also be useful to make them readily available from the press area of the website.

The best archived "press rooms" may also have a selection of images which editors can browse and download to accompany pieces they're writing. And it is also essential to have information about who to contact with queries clearly displayed somewhere in the "press room" or "media centre". This isn't always the case and can be a source of frustration.

Those organisations that take time to build a press room can find they reap a bonus of extra coverage without having to do any extra work. Or, at least, not much.

CHAPTER 13

EVALUATING SUCCESS

The voice on the end of the line will usually be female, young and nervous and the call will go something like this.

Voice: Is that the editor?"

Editor: (Wary) Yes.

Voice: This is Sophie Clutter-Bucket from Boasting & Hype, the PR company. I'm just calling to see if you got the release we sent last week about the new range of cosmetics for cats.

Editor: (prevaricating, for beneath that rough exterior beats a heart of gold) Er, I think it may be in our system.

Sophie: Do you think you might be using it?

Editor: This is the Isle of Arran Shinty Weekly.

Sophie: (without missing a beat) So do you think you'll run the story?

Editor: (spelling it out) Most of our stories are about hairy men hitting each other with sticks. We don't carry stories about cosmetics or cats.

Sophie: (on another planet) If you can't find it, would you like me to e-mail it over again?

Editor: No. Don't do that. Please don't do that. (Slams down telephone handset in despair.)

It's natural that you'll want to know whether a particular publication is going to run your story, but this is not the way to find out. Steve Wright, from Business South East, echoes many journalists when he says: "The biggest pain as an editor is having

25 people a day calling to see if you have used their release. It's impossible to keep a track of what's been used and what's not."

Says Sue Copeman, editor of the magazine StrategicRISK: "Please don't follow up with a phone call." Sue, who receives up to 200 releases a week, adds: "I decide pretty quickly if a release is likely to be interesting and, while I know that PR people want to know if you're going to use the release, I find follow-up calls pretty irritating." Most other journalists echo these sentiments.

So if you can't call the journalists without sending them into despair what can you do to find out whether your stories have made ink? That partly depends on the scale of your press release operation. If you're sending releases at limited frequency to a small number of publications – perhaps newspapers and magazines in your area or a high priority list of trade and technical publications – there's no reason why you shouldn't monitor the contents of each issue yourself.

If you're running a larger release operation, however, that probably won't be viable. You will need to engage the services of a press cuttings agency or, if you're directing your release at radio and tv stations, a broadcast monitoring agency. (The names and contact details of some of these are in appendix two on page 160.) Cuttings agencies employ specially trained readers who search through newspapers and magazines looking for mentions of client companies. A market leader in the field says it monitors 4,300 newspapers and magazines.

Yet although the best cuttings agencies will pick up the majority of the cuttings your organisation receives, some PR people complain they miss cuttings, sometimes important pieces of coverage. It's not surprising. The whole operation relies on human beings reading newspapers and magazines and humans are

fallible. For their part, the cuttings agencies say they're less likely
to miss cuttings if they get a complete list of each publication that
received each release. It also helps to give them a kind of "A list" of
the publications which are especially important to you. The final
backstop is that you can also arrange for these A-list publications
to be sent direct to you and check them yourself.

But as you admire the pile of cuttings on your desk, there may
be another question you ought to be asking yourself. Just what is
the value of all this?

DISCOVERING THE VALUE

You'll have put effort into getting all that press coverage. Is it doing you any good? One way is to evaluate it and find out – but
there are a number of traps in doing that. For a start, how do you
evaluate the value of the coverage? In practice, you might want to
consider one of four different approaches.

Column centimetres

This is the simplest and it's been widely used over the years by
press officers to justify the value of their work. As a simple if crude
measure, it has a certain validity. If you're putting out lots of releases but generating no or little coverage, you're obviously wasting your time. On the other hand, if you're racking up plenty of
column centimetres, you must, presumably, be doing something
right. Measuring the number of column centimetres provides a
benchmark for you to judge how the weight of coverage is moving
from month to month – and it's easy and simple to do.

But it doesn't really tell you much more than the fact you've
been mentioned in the press. It doesn't differentiate between types
of publication – coverage in a small local paper is measured in the

same way as a national. It doesn't explore whether the coverage is positive or negative. It doesn't allow for the fact that your company's mention may be only a passing reference in an otherwise lengthy piece which devotes more coverage to rivals. It doesn't even identify whether the coverage was an incidental mention or the result of your own press campaign. Yet if you don't have the resources to do anything else, it's possibly better than nothing providing you and your colleagues are well aware of its limitations.

Advertising equivalent value

For those who like to know the price of everything (but, perhaps, like Oscar Wilde's cynic, the value of nothing), it's possible to calculate the advertising value equivalent of the press coverage received. The strength of this approach is that it puts a cash value on the results of your press relations activity. There may be sceptics in your organisation who doubt the value of it and see only the costs of the activity, rather than any pay-off. Measuring the column centimetres, then calculating what it would have cost to buy the same space in advertising, gives you a figure you can use in your battles with the sceptics.

This approach does have the merit of attaching different weights to different publications – through the variation in their advertising rates. But it suffers from some of the same faults as measuring column centimetres. Your organisation may only have a small mention in a larger piece and it takes no account of positive or negative coverage. Moreover, most publications discount their advertising rate cards, sometimes heavily, so that calculations using the rate cards give an unrealistically high value to the coverage you've received. Even so, this is an approach which might give a nice warm feeling to people who like looking at financial numbers.

Media evaluation

In the last few years, there has been a considerable growth in the number of specialist companies which offer more sophisticated ways of measuring the value of media coverage. So much so, in fact, that they have formed their own industry association, the Association of Media Evaluation Companies, whose contact details are included in appendix two on page 161.

This growth has taken place largely because the more sophisticated users of media relations realised that they needed to discover just how far their media coverage was supporting their organisation's business objectives or the objectives of specific media campaigns. These specialists have developed sophisticated methodologies designed to evaluate the value of media coverage. The methodology each company uses is unique but it is likely to take account of issues such as the publication in which the coverage appears, the size of the coverage, its position in the publication, whether the organisation's name is mentioned in a headline or standfirst, whether there are pictures, whether the coverage is favourable or unfavourable to the organisation's or campaign's objectives, whether rival organisations are mentioned alongside it and so on. By giving weights to all of these factors and using an algorithm to calculate them, it's possible to produce a measure which, in theory at least, defines how closely your organisation is getting to achieving its objectives through media coverage.

This approach is certainly much more sophisticated than either of the other two and it has the powerful advantage of linking the coverage to attaining business objectives. Yet the measures the evaluation company produces will depend on the methodology and algorithm it uses and whether that provides a true indication of the value your organisation receives is open to debate. Perhaps a different methodology would produce a different measure. In short, the value of this approach depends on agreeing at the outset what the methodology should be and that it will provide a reliable indicator of the value of the media coverage.

And, at the end of the day, while the measurement you get may tell you what the media think about your organisation and its activities, it doesn't tell you how far that coverage has shaped public perceptions about what your organisation does.

Market research

To find out what people think, you may want to consider doing some market research. The Market Research Society, whose contact details are in appendix two on page 161, can provide lists of market research firms that perform attitude surveys. The specialists can help you design a survey which should provide you with information about the positive and negative perceptions people have of your organisation.

But, of course, regular market research is not an inexpensive option. And each survey is only a snapshot in time of public attitudes towards your company. To know whether those perceptions are improving or declining, you need to repeat the research at regular intervals.

Another problem is to know just how far public perceptions about you are shaped by what people read in the media and how much by other factors – such as their personal experience of using your products or services. To some extent, a skilled market research firm can design a piece of research to filter out the impact of media coverage, but this is not a precise science.

So is there a perfect way of evaluating the success of your press releases? Probably not. The four methods mentioned all have their advantages and disadvantages to greater or lesser degrees. The option you choose, if any, depends on the extent of your press operation, the size of your budget – and how much you want to know.

PUTTING PRESS COVERAGE TO WORK

So you've got your column inches and that's it, isn't it? Not necessarily. Organisations that are clever about it can put their press coverage to work in creative ways. Some of the more common are:

Something nice to say. Helpful quotations from positive articles about the company or flattering reviews of products can be lifted and used in the company's own literature, on its website or even in press advertisements. Usually, there is no problem about taking and using a short quotation providing it is properly attributed. If in doubt, ask the publication's permission. But don't doctor sentences – for example, by including a flattering comment made in the first half of the sentence but leaving out a criticism in the second half. This kind of selective quotation can come back to haunt you – not least from the publication that finds its balanced copy twisted for your commercial ends.

Aren't we famous? On the whole, people like to work for organisations that are well thought of and positively written about. So don't forget to circulate your press successes to staff members. In a small company, the simplest way is to pin favourable press cuttings on the staff noticeboard. But you could also photocopy and circulate them – although you will need to comply with photocopying regulations if you want to do this. (For details of photocopying, contact the Authors Licensing and Collecting Society whose details are on page 162.)

This is our life. You also want prospective clients or customers to know that you're an organisation the press respects and takes seriously. So why not compile a book of press cuttings and leave it in reception? Something more useful and informative for callers to flip through while they're waiting for an appointment than a months-old dog-eared magazine.

Reprinted by permission. Some newspapers and magazines offer a reprint service to organisations featured in articles. This is only really useful when your organisation is the sole or main one included in a particular piece – and, of course, when the article presents you in a favourable light. Reprints are often not cheap because the newspapers and magazines see them as a useful supplementary source of revenue, but reprints can become very effective pieces of marketing collateral.

Linked on the web. Some companies provide copies of the most favourable articles on their own website – but permission from the publication concerned is needed before you do this. Others provide web links to those pages on newspaper and magazine websites containing helpful articles. It adds credibility to your site for visitors who may not have logged on to it before. But don't send visitors off to too many other sites – they may find them more interesting than your own.

A final word

Is it all worth it? Could your time be better spent doing something other than drafting and distributing press releases? At the end of the day, press coverage is worthwhile if it helps your organisation to achieve the objectives it has set itself. If it does that, the time you spend reaps multiple benefits.

If you decide that press relations can help your organisation, hopefully this book has given you an insight into what you can do to make your press releases – a key tool in press relations – more effective. Like any activity, you will not achieve good results if you approach press relations in a casual or unprofessional manner. But a well organised and delivered press campaign can produce real business benefits.

And it's great to see your organisation in print.

Appendix i

Useful books

General writing guides:

New Oxford Spelling Dictionary: The Writers' and Editors' Guide to Spelling and Word Division (Oxford University Press). Good dictionary choice for press release writers.

How to Write Well at Work, by Peter Bartram (New Venture Publishing). Published in April 2006. Invaluable companion for the office writer. (www.writewellatwork.co.uk)

Fowler's Modern English Usage by Henry Fowler, Simon Winchester (Oxford Language Classics). The classic witty guide to using English elegantly.

Mind the Gaffe: The Penguin Guide to Common Errors in English, by R L Trask. Does what it says on the cover.

Eats, Shoots and Leaves: the Zero Tolerance Approach to Punctuation, by Lynn Truss (Profile Books). Amusing comments about commas and semi-colons.

Editing and style guides

New Hart's Rules: The Handbook of Style for Writers and Editors, R M Ritter (Adapter), (Oxford University Press). Used for years by editors as their first point of reference.

Copy-Editing: The Cambridge Handbook for Editors, Authors and Publishers by Judith Butcher (Cambridge University Press). All you need to know in this rather pricey book.

Proofreading Plain and Simple by Debra Hart May (Career Press). Straightforward guide to the task.

The Economist Style Guide (The Economist/Profile Books). Handy reference for all those nit-picking style problems.

Appendix 2

Resource centre

Editorial programmes

Companies that provide listings of newspaper and magazine future features include:

FeaturesExec from The Source
Melrose House
42 Dingwall Road
Croydon CR9 2DX
0870 774 0777
www.featuresexec.com

Marketing

Chartered Institute of Marketing
Moor Hall
Cookham
Maidenhead
Berkshire SL6 9QH
Tel: 01628 427500
www.cim.co.uk

Direct Marketing Association
DMA House
70 Margaret Street
London W1W 8SS
020 7291 3300
www.dma.org.uk

Market Research Society
15 Northburgh Street
London EC1V 0JR
020 7490 4911
www.mrs.org.uk

Media evaluation and analysis

Association of Media Evaluation Companies
55 Ramsden Road
London SW12 8RA
020 8675 4442
www.amec.org.uk

Photocopying rights

Authors Licensing and Collecting Society
Marlborough Court
14-18 Holborn
London EC1N 2LE
020 7395 0600
www.alcs.co.uk

Press cuttings

CIS Information Systems
73 Farringdon Road
London EC1M 3JQ
020 7242 5886
www.cisinformation.co.uk

Durrants
Discovery House
28-42 Banner Street
London EC1 8QE
020 7674 0200
www.durrants.co.uk

International Press Cutting Bureau
224/236 Walworth Road
London SE17 1JE
020 7708 2113
www.ipcb.co.uk

Press cutting presentation

Paperclip Partnership
9 The Ashway Centre
Elm Crescent
Kingston-upon-Thames
Surrey KT2 6HH
020 8549 4857
www.paperclippartnership.co.uk

Press release distribution

PR Newswire
209-215 Blackfriars Road
London SE1 8NL
020 7490 8111
www.prnewswire.co.uk

The Source
Melrose House
42 Dingwall Road
Croydon CR9 2DX
0870 774 0777
www.featuresexec.com

Public relations associations

Chartered Institute of Public Relations
32 St James's Square
London SW1Y 4JR
020 7766 3333
www.ipr.org.uk

Public Relations Consultants Association
Willow House
Willow Place
London SW1P 1JH
020 7233 6026
www.prca.org.uk

Publications directory

BRAD
33-39 Bowling Green Lane
London EC1R 0DA
020 7505 8273
www.intellagencia.com

Radio and TV monitoring

Broadcast Monitoring Company
89 Worship Street
London EC2A 2BE
020 7247 1166
www.bmc.co.uk

Romeike & Curtice
Romeike House
290-296 Green Lanes
London N13 5TP
0870 736 0020
www.romeike.com

Regulatory body

UK Listing Authority
25 The North Colonnade
Canary Wharf
London E14 5HS
020 7066 1000
www.fsa.gov.uk

Telephone recording equipment

Retell
53 Thames Street
Sunbury on Thames
Middlesex TW16 5QH
01932 730890
www.retellrecorders.co.uk

INDEX